STRATEGIC
Integration

TIPS, TOOLS, AND TECHNIQUES TO
MOVE BEYOND STRATEGIC PLANNING AND
TRANSFORM YOUR ORGANIZATION

Gabriel Eckert & Bob Harris
FASAE, CAE   CAE

★asae®
association
management
press

WASHINGTON, DC

The authors have worked diligently to ensure that all information in this book is accurate as of the time of publication and consistent with standards of good practice in the general management community. As research and practice advance, however, standards may change. For this reason it is recommended that readers evaluate the applicability of any recommendations in light of particular situations and changing standards.

ASAE: The Center for Association Leadership
1575 I Street, NW
Washington, DC 20005-1103
Phone: (202) 626-2723; (888) 950-2723 outside metropolitan Washington, DC area
Fax: (202) 371-8315
Email: books@asaecenter.org

We connect great ideas and great people to inspire leadership and achievement in the association community.

Keith C. Skillman, CAE, Vice President, Publications and Knowledge Integration,
    ASAE: The Center for Association Leadership
Baron Williams, CAE, Senior Director, Book and Information Publishing,
    ASAE: The Center for Association Leadership

Cover and text design by Troy Scott Parker, Cimarron Design

This book is available at a special discount when ordered in bulk quantities. For information, contact the ASAE Member Service Center at (202) 371-0940. A complete catalog of titles is available on the ASAE website at www.asaecenter.org.

ISBN-13: 978-0-88034-392-3

Printed in the United States of America.

10 9 8 7 6 5 4 3 2 1

Contents

Foreword

Human history is experiencing a unique and unprecedented convergence of life-altering variables in an increasingly rapid explosion. At this exact moment, a new generation of association leaders is emerging for whom an effective way to deploy strategic thinking, planning, and execution requires an ever more adaptive responsiveness to stay relevant. Simplicity is being demonstrated as a hallmark of cutting edge associations, those that seek to magnify and leverage their influence through laser focus.

Gabriel Eckert, FASAE, CAE, chief executive officer, consultant, and co-author of ASAE's bestselling book *From Insight to Action*, has partnered with Bob Harris, CAE, author and international consultant, to share a tool that emphasizes the power of simplicity in strategic thinking, planning, and execution. An essential complement to enrich preparation for your next strategic implementation, it is packed with visuals, case studies, and questions to lead your association through appropriate adaptation.

Having designed and led an association transformation early in my career, without the benefit of an implementation reference guide of this type, it's refreshing to have a template capture the essence of how to move beyond the strategic planning retreat to ongoing transformative implementation. With a nod to those elements that continue to be an integral part of the process, *Strategic Integration* tees up practitioners to make a strategic plan come alive, alter culture, execute seamlessly, and reinvigorate regularly.

As both a practicing association CEO and strategic consultant, I have witnessed three common factors challenging our 21st century leadership: accelerating complexity; speed of change overwhelming decision makers; and clarity suffering from attempts to address and accomplish too much. As the significance of our leadership intensifies and the magnitude of our decisions' impact increases, one of the essential points of mastery for a board and CEO partnership is to determine what really matters and to ignore the swirling chaos of distractors. *Strategic Integration* helps board and staff zoom in on fewer, yet bolder, strategies—communicating, testing, adjusting, staying vigilant, and being tolerant of calculated risks as a teacher—all essential components for organizational transformation. Marrying these with role clarity, aligned operational excellence, engaging storytelling, iterative innovation, and systematic sunsetting creates the potential for organizations to live consistently in strategic intent.

Responding to our diverse members' perceived challenges and views of their association's role—as a community, problem solver, and advocate—is critical and multi-faceted. Simplicity and alignment point the user to one method of engaging effectively to answer with focused, continuous impact. Translation of this strategic practice into an association's culture, with the appropriate pacing of change, encourages us not to default back to what is familiar and to deploy strategy that passes the reasonableness test.

For the novice, *Strategic Integration* is a blueprint. For the seasoned, it's a reminder. For the tempted, desiring the comfort of old habits, it's a cautionary tale. For the new board member, it's a Sherpa. For the aspiring CEO, it's a flashlight. For the mentor, it's a tool. For the facilitator, it's a resource. In other words, *Strategic Integration* is an essential addition to your library for strategic implementation in the 21st century.

- Cynthia Mills, FASAE, CAE, CMC
  The Leaders' Haven

Introduction

There is, perhaps, no competency that leaders know their organization needs more than strategic planning. Each year, organizations invest countless dollars and hours building and revising strategic plans. Why is it, then, that so many plans fail? They fail to transform organizations. They fail to inspire individuals. Or, in many cases, they fail to be implemented altogether. What do the most effective organizations do—beyond strategic planning—to ensure their strategy is achieved?

Highly effective leaders think differently. They understand that strategic planning isn't simply building a plan—it is a state of mind, a way of being, and a continual, organic conversation about the future.

Leaders also understand that organizational structure and systems, much more than the process of planning, often dictate failure or success. This book challenges leaders to think beyond strategic planning and focus on the organizational foundations necessary to successfully implement strategy: Simplicity, Creative Communication, Operational Excellence, Maintaining Focus, Absolute Alignment, Iterative Innovation, Systematic Sunsetting, and building a Strategy-Driven Culture.

To reinforce these concepts, each chapter ends with several questions to consider. These questions are designed to encourage dialogue among organizational leaders around how to implement the ideas presented in this book.

In exploring the topic of strategic planning and implementation, the authors bring a combined six decades of experience in association management, strategic planning, and organizational leadership. They also bring a balanced perspective, having served in the role of staff, volunteer, and consultant for hundreds of nonprofit organizations. Theories proposed in the book are grounded in research of contemporary texts in strategic planning as well as case study and qualitative research from dozens of organizations engaging in strategic planning throughout the world.

Overall, the book is designed to be simple, yet comprehensive. And to ensure that *Strategic Integration* is more than just theory, this book includes an extensive Resources section, featuring several tips, tools, and techniques designed to make the content both practical and practiced in association management. *Strategic Integration* empowers leaders to transform their organizations, inspire others, and ensure that their strategic plan is implemented effectively.

Chapter 1

Strategic Integration

For many organizations, creating a strategic plan is like crossing a finish line. With a new plan in place, it is widely assumed that the organization will systematically implement the priorities within it, and as a result be successful. In reality, once a strategic plan is crafted, the journey has just begun. The success of that journey largely depends not just on strategic planning, but on the *Strategic Integration* of the plan into the organization.

The concepts explored in this book provide a model for leaders to integrate their strategic plan into the very fiber of the organization they serve. While the book is largely written from the perspective of the nonprofit sector, the concepts and strategies are transferable beyond that sector. *Strategic Integration* also applies broadly in the nonprofit sector, assisting trade associations, individual membership organizations, chambers of commerce, philanthropic organizations, nongovernmental organizations, and others.

So how do organizations move beyond strategic planning? By engaging in *Strategic Integration*, which leverages the following concepts within an organization to create strategic awareness and focus:

- Condense a strategic plan into a simple, easy to understand format;

- Communicate creatively, using stories, mantras, and strong visual elements;

- Ensure operational excellence through sound planning and use of automation;

- Align member and staff resources to achieve strategic priorities;

- Embrace iterative innovation;

- Systematically sunset programs and services to create capacity for change and growth; and

- Create a strategy-driven culture that includes a shared definition of success, engages in continuous learning, and celebrates success.

Individually, these concepts are simple. Collectively, they are transformational. Translating the concepts into action is a team effort. The chief staff officer and staff at all levels, as well as members of the board of directors and volunteers serving in a variety of capacities each have a role to play. When applied consistently within an organization, the *Strategic Integration* model affects how an organization shares its vision for the future; how it operates, both at the foundational and strategic levels; and ultimately, it influences how the organization is at its core, by embracing a strategy-driven culture that fulfills its mission and values.

Strategic Integration		
How We Share	**How We Operate**	**How We Are**
Simplicity	*Operational Excellence*	*Strategy-Driven Culture*
Creative Communication	*Maintain Focus*	
	Absolute Alignment	
	Iterative Innovation	
	Systematic Sunsetting	

How We Share

Simplicity has a way of cutting through the clutter of an increasingly complex world. *Strategic Integration* challenges organizational leaders to rethink how they compose their strategic plans and how they communicate them to their stakeholders. Distilling lengthy plans into their essence creates streamlined messaging and enhanced comprehension. Essentially, *Simplicity* sells the strategy. This approach, combined with *Creative Communication,* in which the art of storytelling is combined with the use of mantras, provides leaders with an engaging way to share their vision of the future. Adding strong visual elements into the mix of how strategic plans are communicated further builds a compelling case for the necessity of priorities included in an organization's strategic plan.

How We Operate

Organizations need to be well operated before their strategic plans can be consistently and most effectively implemented. Creating both operational and strategic priority implementation plans, while leveraging automation, help staff ensure the operations of the organization they serve are performing well. Organizations that add to this a holistic understanding of the ecosystem in which they operate achieve *Operational Excellence* and position themselves in a way that increases the odds of success in implementing strategic priorities.

The number of ideas for new programs and services among volunteers and staff in a nonprofit will always exceed the organization's ability to implement them. Inevitably, strategic plans also include a surplus of ideas beyond an organization's ability to implement in a single year. Therefore, leaders must intentionally decide to focus on a limited number of strategic priorities in any given timeframe and monitor progress toward achieving them. This focus, however, should not be rigid. The art of understanding when to be flexible to capitalize on an unforeseen opportunity or to guard against unexpected changes in circumstances is also key for leaders. Organizations that are *Maintaining Focus* on a few strategic priorities at a time and routinely monitoring progress, while exhibiting sufficient flexibility, position themselves well to achieve strategic success.

To achieve their strategic priorities, leaders must also ensure that organizational resources are aligned appropriately. The *Absolute Alignment* of both human capital and financial resources is essential for success. To effectively implement a strategic plan, boards of directors must empower staff and volunteers to carry out their vision. Asking individuals and work groups to focus on tasks that align with their unique skills, knowledge, and relationships engages them appropriately in work supporting a strategic priority. Additionally, ensuring there is a shared understanding of the specific roles volunteers and staff assume in the work of an association builds clarity and reduces conflict.

Not every big idea needs to be perfected before it is implemented. Many strategic plans include big, bold ideas for programs, member benefits, or services. And many organizations struggle with perfecting these initiatives before they are launched. Learning from the technology sector, nonprofit organizations are increasingly implementing strategic priorities in iterations. Organizations build and deliver a prototype and then build and improve on it in future iterations. This approach creates a cycle of learning, continual improvement, and innovation. Often times, this *Iterative Innovation* also increases the speed of delivery of new strategic initiatives.

It is easy for nonprofit organizations to hold on to underperforming programs or services, with declining value propositions, for too long. Inertia keeps them in place. Without questioning the status quo, leaders often don't realize how much organizational capacity is tied up in programs and services that are beyond their useful life— and their continued operation comes at the expense of capacity for new, strategic priorities. Building an ongoing plan for the review and *Systematic Sunsetting* of programs and services is essential to ensuring adequate resources are available for the development of new initiatives included in a strategic plan.

How We Are

Strategic planning should not only be an annual exercise, it should be a way of being. Building a *Strategy-Driven Culture* in an organization is critical for long-term success. But what is the definition of success? This is one of the most fundamental questions a board of directors must ask, and the answer has a profound and lasting impact.

Associations must redefine how they measure success. The degree to which organizational success is defined by operational metrics must diminish. Rather, organizations should largely define success as effectively implementing strategic priorities. Over time, if strategic priorities are correctly based on stakeholder needs and preferences, operational metrics should improve as a side effect.

This type of strategic focus requires members and staff to engage in continuous learning, and to authentically appreciate contributions from individuals who serve the organization. Celebrating success reinforces the *Strategy-Driven Culture* as people feel appreciated and can see how their efforts contributed to accomplishing strategic priorities.

Strategic Integration

Comprehensively integrating the concepts of *Strategic Integration* into an organization helps leaders move beyond strategic planning. It creates a heightened awareness of and support for strategic initiatives. It strengthens stakeholder engagement. And, importantly, it dramatically increases the odds of success in implementing a strategic plan.

Chapter 2

. . . .

Simplicity

The benefits of simplification are many: less clutter, increased organization, better focus, and enhanced comprehension of ideas, just to name a few. Why, then, are so many strategic plans still so unnecessarily complex?

The most effective strategic plans are visionary, yet concise; bold, yet brief; expansive in ideas, yet limited in words. Today, too many strategic plans are lengthy, complex documents that fail to effect significant change, much less generate any sort of buy-in from members and other stakeholders. Big ideas don't require a large transcript. Concise, multi-year strategic plans are easier to read, follow, and implement. They are also more easily conveyed to individuals outside of the board of directors or strategic planning committee.

Many strategic planning exercises produce large plan documents that include multiple pages of background information. This information can provide context for the strategies developed, including details such as environmental scanning, underlying assumptions, and organizational values. This can be helpful for boards and staff to maintain a shared understanding of the plan, particularly as individuals in key roles change over time. However, the length of these documents can also cause some organizations to lose sight of the strategic priorities that have been chosen for implementation.

To increase focus on strategic priorities, many boards create a simplified version of their strategic plan, retaining the longer version primarily for an annual review. This can prove to be quite useful for most organizations; but to really drive success in focusing on strategic priorities, some organizations are finding ways to simplify even further. Imagine a strategic plan that fits on a single page. Simpler still, what if a strategic plan could be made to fit on a single business card? Here are two organizations that have found a great deal of success by using these approaches.

New Hampshire Automobile Dealers Association (NHADA) transformed its eight-page strategic plan into a single-page plan. This simplification helped the association to both focus more easily and monitor progress more clearly. The association also designated each of its strategic steps (priorities) to be completed in a specific year, over a three-year period. This approach helped the board to better understand the necessary flow of implementing the plan and also maintain consensus on the intended timeline.

The Florida Academy of Family Physicians took the concept of simplification a step further. The organization shrunk its strategic plan to the size of a business card. The two-sided card clearly featured the organization's mission, vision, and values as well as its strategic goals. Strategic priorities and progress were tracked by the board of directors in a separate document.

The plan was printed in business card size. The card also included a website address where a more extensive version of the strategic plan was featured. The business cards were given to each member of the board of directors to remind them of the organization's strategic focus. Directors were also able to give the business card to members, prospective members, and others if asked about the strategic direction of the organization. In doing so, the miniature strategic plan became more widely read and understood than previous, lengthy plans the organization had produced.

Goals, Plans, and Strategies (GPS)

Mission: Protecting the motor vehicle industry's interest at the State House and helping grow your business.

Membership Excellence	Public Relations	Leadership Development	Advocacy	Education & Resources
Provide essential services to grow and retain membership.	*Promote the industry's positive image & impact.*	*Maintain a structure, workforce, and finances to sustain a powerful association.*	*Continue to be the industry's trusted leader and voice.*	*Be the preeminent source for compliance education & info.*
STRATEGIC STEPS	**STRATEGIC STEPS**	**STRATEGIC STEPS**	**STRATEGIC STEPS**	**STRATEGIC STEPS**
▸ Sharpen the endorsement process (Year 1)	▸ Promote our scholarship giving (Year 1)	▸ Examine ROI on Association services (Year 1)	▸ Develop a legislative scorecard and questionnaire (Year 1)	▸ Promote employment legal hotline (Year 1)
▸ Create a uniform retail Installment Contract and P&S Agreement (Year 1)	▸ Explore endorsing safety campaign (Year 1 & 2)	▸ Restructure and define committees to align with Strategic Plan (Year 1)	▸ Increase lobbying strength (Year 1)	▸ Promote online education (Year 1)
▸ Explore Self-insured P&C (Year 1)	▸ Measure and promote economic impact of NHADA members (Year 2)	▸ Engage more volunteer leaders (Year 1, 2, & 3)	▸ Strengthen State and Federal PACs (Year 1)	▸ Survey members for education needs (Year 1)
▸ Host a NH Auto Show (Year 2)	▸ Measure and promote community service impact of NHADA members (Year 2)	▸ Ensure adequate staffing levels (Year 1, 2, & 3)	▸ Develop a grassroots ambassador program (Year 1)	▸ Host annual meeting, golf outing, town meetings, and conventions (Year 1, 2, & 3)
▸ Assess Member needs for products and services (Year 1)	▸ Increase social media footprint of NHADA (Year 2)	▸ Update governing documents (Year 1)	▸ Work with associations in New England (Year 1)	▸ Create a legal compliance manual (Year 2)
▸ Create EVR program for NH (Year 1, 2, & 3, iteratively launched)			▸ Be vigilant and proactive at the State House (Year 1)	▸ Update website (Year 3)
▸ Create a marketing plan (Year 2)				▸ Consider creating self-audit kits & Compliance Audits (Year 3)
▸ Examine the dues structure (Year 2)				
▸ Increase member participation in events (Year 2)				

Source: New Hampshire Automobile Dealers Association. Reprinted with permission.

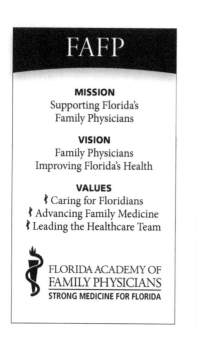

FAFP

MISSION
Supporting Florida's
Family Physicians

VISION
Family Physicians
Improving Florida's Health

VALUES
❧ Caring for Floridians
❧ Advancing Family Medicine
❧ Leading the Healthcare Team

FLORIDA ACADEMY OF
FAMILY PHYSICIANS
STRONG MEDICINE FOR FLORIDA

Goal 1 **Advocacy**
Be the leading advocate for family
physicians and the specialty of family
medicine in Florida to promote
healthcare excellence for patients.

Goal 2 **Education**
Be the premier resource for
CME, knowledge exchange,
and professional development
through the FAFP Foundation.

Goal 3 **Practice Improvement and
Career Enhancement**
Enhance and support members'
abilities to fulfill practice and career
goals and pursue work-life balance.

Goal 4 **Member Engagement and
Leadership**
Emphasize and enhance the
value of a united profession
through membership.

www.fafpstrategicplan.com

Source: Florida Academy of Family Physicians. Reprinted with permission.

So, what are the common characteristics and benefits of a simplified strategic plan? Simple strategic plans boil down complex documents into their essence, in a format that is easy to distribute, read, and comprehend. And the benefits are many: they become easier to use, and therefore more likely to be widely used by organizational leaders; they increase clarity around an organization's strategic focus; and they are easier to communicate and remember.

"Simplicity is the ultimate sophistication," Leonardo da Vinci once said. Applying the concept of simplicity to strategic plans not only makes them more sophisticated, but stronger as well.

There's another common saying that "less is more." Arguably, one of the most significant and well-known speeches in American history is Abraham Lincoln's Gettysburg Address. At 272 words, it was delivered in less than three minutes. It was concise, simple, and powerful. It proves the point that not all grand visions have to be accompanied by verbosity. The quality of a strategic plan, like the quality of Lincoln's address, is found not in the length of the document but in the power of its ideas.

Simplicity, however, does not imply lack of a need for planning. Prior to implementing strategic priorities, a strategic priority implementation plan (detailed on page 29) should be developed by staff to translate strategic priorities into specific, measurable tactics. However, for the board of directors to be able to effectively communicate an association's strategy, simplicity will always trump complexity.

Questions to Consider

- What is the essence of our strategic plan?

- How can we create a simple version of our strategic plan to share with others?

- In what ways would using a simplified version of our strategic plan more clearly articulate our strategy?

- To what audiences can we distribute a simplified version of our strategic plan?

Chapter 3

Creative Communication

At its best, a strategic plan will captivate the imagination of stakeholders, inspiring them to engage with and support the plan, and become advocates for change. But a strategic plan will never be at its best if it is not effectively communicated. Communication strategies must include more than bullet points listing strategic objectives. It must be more than simply listing how the organization will grow or evolve. The most effective messaging highlights how stakeholders will be affected, how lives will be changed, or how communities will benefit. Essentially, the messaging needs to focus on how the stakeholder is positively affected, not on how the organization will benefit.

There are three primary ways in which organizations can accomplish this: storytelling, mantras, and visual communication. Using these methods makes it easier for others to see how the plan will have a positive impact on them, or to advance the things they care most about. This means that they are more likely to buy in to the strategic plan. Associations that utilize any, or ideally all, of these methods of communication will find the greatest success in achieving their objectives.

Storytelling

Since the dawn of time, humans have been using stories to convey information. Stories help to form a connection between the information being presented, its meaning or message, and the audience reading or listening. People naturally care more about information, and find it easier to draw lessons from it, if it is presented in the form of a story. Smart association leaders understand this, and use this power of storytelling to their advantage. This can be particularly useful when conveying strategic goals.

Organizations need to frame their messaging to align with what motivates their audience, and an incredibly effective way to do that is through telling a compelling story. The words chosen when communicating obviously impact how an audience receives and understands a message. Oftentimes, organizations communicate their strategic plan in terms of bullet points, abstract goals, or framed as outcomes that highlight benefits the organization itself will receive. This approach focuses more on the organization's desire to communicate its strategy, rather than on communicating how the strategy will have a positive impact on the intended audience.

To effectively communicate a strategic priority, association leaders must verbally paint a picture to illustrate how the organization's actions will positively affect those to whom they are communicating. Effective stories have four qualities in common. They are attention-grabbing, relatable, compelling, and action-oriented.

A powerful story begins with setting the stage in a way that grabs—and holds—the attention of the audience. It is presented in a way in which listeners can easily relate to the story that is being told. This underscores the importance of knowing your audience. A strong story is also compelling in that it generates an emotional response for the listener. Effective storytellers use a combination of data and anecdote to achieve this response. And finally, an effective story ends with a call to action, which helps focus an emotional response from a listener into tangible outcomes.

American Forests, a nonprofit organization focused on protecting and restoring forests, enthusiastically uses storytelling to advance its strategic initiatives. In fact, the organization has integrated the use of stories into virtually everything it does.

From public speeches to private conversations, in its print publications as well as its website, and through social media to video production, the organization continually frames its messaging in the context of a story.

Staff continually invests time in uncovering the core narratives of the organization. This work includes finding and developing the most inspiring stories about the organization's work—things like protecting grizzly bear habitat in the Northern Rockies, restoring forests in the West destroyed by massive forest fires, and transforming cities by expanding tree canopy cover and green space.

But it also includes stories that provide a narrative that strengthens the organizational culture. These include stories of how the organization rebuilt itself after a tough patch in the early 2000s; member trips tracking wolves across Yellowstone or seeing the monarch butterfly migration in Mexico; and public relations wins like major media coverage it has received, a series of events with actor Ryan Reynolds, a mention by Oprah Winfrey on her TV show, and other positive attention. These stories help reinforce a sense of momentum and accomplishment for both board and staff.

This comprehensive use of stories has resulted in unified messaging and positioning of the organization across its communications channels. And it has translated into enhanced engagement of members and increased support from donors.

The organization has also effectively used storytelling in implementing priorities from its strategic plan. Historically, the organization would produce fact-based materials and presentations to create awareness of and advance its strategic priorities. Over time, organizational leaders realized there was an opportunity to better engage others in support of strategic initiatives by using stories. As a result, the organization focused on creating content that was both informational and inspiring.

American Forests first used its story-centric approach with a single strategic plan priority, a new initiative designed to expand habitat for endangered species. The initiative focused on specific forest ecosystems, selected because of their significant biodiversity value, where the organization had a long history of restoration work, and where making a longer-term commitment could play a transformational role in ecosystem recovery.

Preceding the launch of the program, staff developed a story around each ecosystem. The stories were framed around either communities of people who live near the forest or around a charismatic species—from the ocelot, a beautiful wild cat in Texas, to the gopher tortoise, a remarkable resourceful keystone species in the Southeast. Building the stories this way helped the audience form an emotional connection with the targeted ecosystems and visualize the impact they could make by participating in the Wildlands for Wildlife program. This emotional connection was then reinforced with logic by utilizing facts and statistics relating to those stories after they had been told. The approach leveraged both right- and left-brain thinking in stakeholders and better inspired them to take action in support of the program. In essence, it helped the organization reach people in a deep, comprehensive, and authentic way.

American Forests' leaders have identified three ways in which the use of storytelling has positively impacted the implementation of its strategic priorities. It has increased the number of members and stakeholders who support strategic initiatives. It inspired staff to think more deeply about how their job functions affect organizational strategy. And, perhaps most significantly, it has equipped board members and staff with tools to better and more effectively communicate.

In another segment of the nonprofit sector, FarmHouse Fraternity also integrated storytelling into one of its strategic priorities. The fraternity had a strategic initiative to rebrand the organization. This included updating the fraternity's visual elements, including a new website, logo, and revisions to its print and electronic communications vehicles. As is typically the case, the organization also created a new style guide to ensure visual and grammatical consistency with the new brand.

THE NEW **FARMHOUSE** SHIELD

9 LINES
The 9 fraternity principles, and a nod to the historic
heritage and agricultural roots of the fraternity.

SHIELD
Conveys fraternity, contemporary update
to the historic shape of the crest

WHITE SASH / 3 STARS
Key historical element from the crest

GREEN, WHITE, GOLD COLORS
Represents the breadth of the member experience:
Green—New Members, White—Alumni Members,
Gold—Chapter Members

Source: FarmHouse Fraternity. Reprinted with permission.

The organization also took the branding initiative a step further by creating not just a style guide, but also a story guide. The guide included key messages for organizational leaders to use when discussing the fraternity, its services, and the new brand. It explained the fraternity's values and how the new visual elements symbolize important aspects of the organization. The graphic above shows how the organization explained the visual elements of a new organizational logo that was created through the rebranding effort. This, combined, with other aspects of the guide ensured consistency in key messages organizational leaders used, and created more strategic alignment among its chapters' websites and other communications platforms.

These two examples, American Forests and FarmHouse Fraternity, from different segments of the nonprofit sector illuminate the importance of and value in using storytelling related to the strategic priorities of an organization.

Mantras

For centuries, spiritual leaders have taught the value of using mantras. A mantra is a word or phrase, repeated frequently and internally in the mind of an individual that is considered to be capable of creating transformation. Repeated throughout years, the mantra becomes more than just words; its meaning becomes a way of life.

The use of mantras in a slightly different form can also have powerful effects in association management, enabling leaders to create change within an organization. If association leaders develop a few short, simple sentences or phrases related to their strategic plan, and find ways to routinely work them into conversation, particularly with members and staff, over time, transformation will begin. In time, a common language and vision of governance and strategy will be created within the organization.

The Building Owners and Managers Association of Georgia (BOMA Georgia) provides an example of using mantras to accomplish the goals in their strategic plan, as well as to create positive change.

After conducting market research, the organization discovered something that it had anecdotally known to be true: corporate budgets for training were cut significantly during the most recent recession, and since the economic recovery, funding for real estate professionals' education remained below its historic levels. This had occurred during a time when there were rapid advances in building technology, newly developed best practices in environmental sustainability and high performance management, and changing preferences among tenants for space use. And while the association's research showed a decline in corporate funding for continuing education, it also revealed an increased need for training among members and other industry stakeholders.

In response, the association's strategic plan included development of new educational programs, real estate research initiatives, and the creation of a new scholarship program. To meet these needs, a new 501(c)(3) foundation was established. This, however, led to its own challenge: how to generate funding for the new foundation. Given that corporate budgets were already tight, how would an appeal for foundation funding be successful? And how could the foundation best appeal to individuals to make tax-deductible donations in support of the foundation's mission? The answer was found both through storytelling, and the use of mantras.

When communicating to businesses, the foundation identified the need for research in the industry, and positioned itself as the entity that could best meet this need. In essence, the foundation's mantra that it repeated to these businesses was that new research produced by the foundation would provide new tools that "transform the way you do business."

When making an appeal to individuals to give to the foundation, messaging revolved around storytelling, using examples of fellow real estate professionals who needed greater access to education. Specifically, it crafted stories that its target audience could relate to. These stories demonstrated how foundation scholarships help real estate professionals get the education they need so that they can better manage and operate the buildings in which they work. This helps individuals advance their career, while also increasing the employee's value to their company, translating into a higher likelihood of raises, bonuses, and promotions. The short mantra was "foundation scholarships advance careers."

The combination of storytelling and consistent use of mantras was the key to success for BOMA Georgia. After a few years, research conducted by the association showed that members and donors connected the work of the foundation with helping individuals advance their careers, and saw the foundation research as a key in transforming the way they do business. As a result, the foundation exceeded its fundraising targets, research initiatives were well received, and enrollment in educational programs supported by foundation scholarships more than doubled. So how did the organization decide to publicize its success? By returning to its mantras, reminding the industry that the foundation is "transforming the way you do business and advancing careers."

One of the most rewarding outcomes of the use of these mantras for BOMA Georgia has been hearing members repeat—spontaneously and in their own words—the mantras back to association leaders, and with others, in conversation. The mantras have helped to improve the association and its foundation, and create a shared vision of organizational strategy.

The Mantra as Message

There are many other adaptations of mantras that can be useful for associations. Creating short sentences related to the organization's value proposition and then distributing them to members can turn members into association evangelists, communicating the organization's value and benefits to potential members.

When the Green Chamber of the South was founded, it leveraged mantras from the start in order to help its board members become organizational evangelists. It can be difficult for new nonprofit organizations to clearly and consistently communicate who they are and what they do. Essentially, since it had never existed before, the organization had the challenge of creating awareness of both its mission and services to audiences who may still not even know it exists.

In response to this challenge, the Green Chamber of the South distilled its mission and services into two mantras and then printed them on business card size handouts that its board members could give to prospective members when discussing the organization. This helped the organization achieve consistency in messaging, equipped board members with mantra-style talking points, and provided prospective members with a small, printed reminder of the organization's mission and services that was easy to keep and remember.

> ### The Green Chamber of the South
> brings together businesses across the Southeast to promote growth, innovation, and success of sustainability.
>
> Join us on the first Wednesday of each month for an informal networking lunch for anyone interested in Sustainable Business in the Metro Atlanta area.
> More detail: www.greencs.org/events/greenwednesdays
>
> NETWORK ▪ EXPOSURE ▪ EDUCATION ▪ GROWTH

Source: Green Chamber of the South. Reprinted with permission.

This tactic helped board members to consistently position the organization as "bringing together businesses across the Southeast to promote growth, innovation, and success of sustainability" through the networking and education the organization provides. It also laid the foundation for membership growth and engagement in the chamber's monthly meetings as board members spread a consistent message through their individual conversations.

There are many other uses for mantras. They can be leveraged during a re-branding effort. Developing a few concise mantras can quickly turn association leaders into brand ambassadors, equipping them with the resources they need to effectively communicate the value of the organization's new brand.

In addition, mantras can help individuals in developing key messages in preparation for media interviews, ensuring the association's main points are properly—and consistently—communicated to the public. They also assist in maintaining focus during the interview, as well as making for excellent pull quotes and sound bites.

Developing and using mission-centric mantras enhances the work of association leaders. These short, simple sentences, used routinely and systematically—in conversation, print, electronic communications, video, and social media—can transform an association and create positive, effective change.

Visual Communication

It is often said that a picture is worth a thousand words. If that's true, then imagine how much more effectively a strategic plan can be communicated through visual representation of its text.

In fact, according to the Social Science Research Network, 65 percent of people are visual learners.[1] And visual elements have been proven to increase comprehension and retention of information.[2]

There is not just a single way to unlock the power of visual communication when it comes to communicating a strategic plan. Organizations use visual communications in a variety of ways. The following are a few examples of how various approaches to visually communicating strategic plans have led diverse organizations to increased levels of success.

The Montana Society of Certified Public Accountants (MSCPA) created a visual element to accompany its one-page strategic plan. It is shown on the next page.

---

[1] https://papers.ssrn.com/sol3/papers.cfm?abstract_id=587201
[2] http://web.stanford.edu/~rhorn/a/recent/artclNSFVisualLangv.pdf

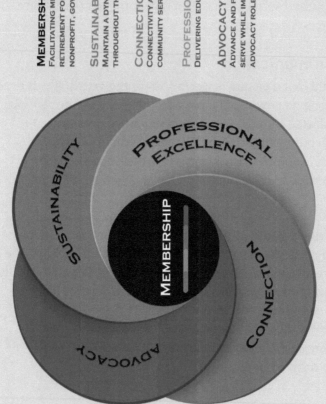

MEMBERSHIP—YOUR PROFESSIONAL HOME
FACILITATING MEMBER SUCCESS FROM ENTRY THROUGH RETIREMENT FOR ALL MEMBERS, INCLUDING BUSINESS, INDUSTRY, NONPROFIT, GOVERNMENT, PUBLIC PRACTICE AND EDUCATORS.

SUSTAINABILITY
MAINTAIN A DYNAMIC ORGANIZATION AND ENSURE WE EXIST THROUGHOUT THE NEXT 100 YEARS

CONNECTION
CONNECTIVITY AND COMMUNICATIONS THROUGH CHAPTERS, COMMUNITY SERVICE AND PUBLIC RELATIONS

PROFESSIONAL EXCELLENCE
DELIVERING EDUCATION AND RESOURCES

ADVOCACY
ADVANCE AND PROTECT THE PROFESSION AND THE PEOPLE WE SERVE WHILE IMPROVING MEMBER AWARENESS OF THE SOCIETY'S ADVOCACY ROLE.

MSCPA
Montana Society
of Certified Public Accountants

Source: Montana Society of CPAs (MSCPA). Reprinted with permission.

What comes to mind when seeing this strong visual element? How quick and easy is it to understand the primary focus of the organization? How might a member—or potential member—of the association feel when seeing this visual?

Now, imagine this communication without the graphic element, leaving only the text to its right. Try placing a hand over the graphic and looking only at the text. How does that feel? What's different about the message that's communicated? How is the impact changed? This shows the power of visual communication and underscores how important it is for organizations to develop new ways of expressing their strategic plan and priorities.

MSCPA's use of this graphic element alongside the goals in its strategic plan increased member awareness of the association's core focus. It also reinforced, in a powerful way, the association's structure as a member-centric organization.

Building on this concept, the Global Cold Chain Alliance (GCCA) created a visual cover page for its strategic plan. The graphic GCCA created is so powerful that one does need not to read the entire

Source: Global Cold Chain Alliance. Reprinted with permission.

strategic plan in order to fully understand the organization's purpose and strategic direction.

The graphic, with limited text and strong visual elements, quickly conveys the purpose and priorities of the organization. In fact, the visual communication is so strong that it clearly communicates the essence of the organization and its strategy in a way that even those who are not familiar with the organization, or the industry it serves, can easily understand what it does.

A different, yet equally impactful, example of visual communication is from The Pearland Chamber of Commerce. Contrasted with the MSCPA example, the Pearland Chamber example shows another way in which the key elements of a strategic plan can be communicated. The organization developed a visual representation of how the strategic plan fulfills its core purpose of being "The Voice of Business" for their community. With

Source: Pearland Chamber of Commerce. Reprinted with permission.

this graphic, it is easy for stakeholders to quickly understand the four ways in which the chamber serves them.

The chamber's limited use of text and the connectivity of the four strategic themes of the organization is a powerful visual representation of how the chamber fulfills its purpose. Anchored by a graphic representation of a community, it also visually reinforces the chamber's role in serving as "the voice of business." Imagine how much less impactful this communication effort would be if, instead of single words, the organization opted to include a litany of bullet points explaining how the chamber makes a difference in the community.

The Florida Swimming Pool Association (FSPA) used a different approach to communicating its strategic plan. It used photographs of scenes that are familiar to its members, and then used those images to draw them in to reading the plan. The organization took this effort further by dramatically enlarging the plan and placing it at a prominent location during its trade show. Doing so increased awareness of the association's strategy and generated conversation among trade show attendees about the direction of the organization. The decision to be so public in promoting FSPA's strategic plan also increased the association's accountability to achieving its goals,

Source: Florida Swimming Pool Association. Reprinted with permission.

because its members could clearly see what to expect in the years ahead.

FSPA's public display is a reminder that strategic plans don't belong on a shelf or in the cloud. To create consensus around—and even excitement for—the strategic direction of an organization, it is essential to visually publicize strategic initiatives in as many ways as possible.

As is evident from these examples, there are many ways to visually communicate a strategic plan. The examples also underscore the critical importance of leveraging strong visual elements when communicating strategic plans and priorities. While each of these organizations used a different method, the impact they achieved was similar: a clear and powerfully presented strategy.

Questions to Consider

• What pictures come to mind when thinking about our strategic plan?

• What visual elements can be used to reflect the key areas of our strategic plan?

• How can we increase the visibility of our strategic plan?

• How can we utilize video to advance our association's strategic priorities?

Chapter 4

Operational Excellence

Operational excellence is the foundation that is necessary for strategic success. It is the ability for an organization to efficiently and effectively follow through on its commitments. And it is found in every association that is well managed.

Since the responsibility for management of an association falls on the chief staff officer (CSO), it is the CSO's opportunity and obligation to ensure the organization achieves *Operational Excellence*. This can be accomplished to a large extent through the alignment of staff, volunteer efforts, and financial resources, but also through the systematic use of operational plans, strategic priority implementation plans, and—increasingly—automation.

Operational Planning

Operational plans define the routine activities of an organization at a tactical level, and then incorporate deadlines and assign responsibility for carrying out each of those activities. In associations, the most common operational plans include marketing, communications, membership, events, education, finance, and other areas of operation.

While it is obvious that well-crafted and well-executed plans lead to *Operational Excellence*, what may not be so obvious is that operational planning is the foundation to achieving strategic success. Operational plans provide a number of benefits, in that they

- result in more efficient use of volunteer and staff time;
- streamline operational activities;
- provide consistency and reliability in operations; and
- build trust among members and staff that key operational activities will occur on time and with standardized quality.

This case study from a national trade association, which shall remain anonymous, magnifies the importance of developing and using solid operational plans, and demonstrates how they affect strategic initiatives.

This association had spent nearly a year crafting a new strategic plan. Through focus groups, research, input from chapter leaders, and strategic planning sessions with its board of directors, the association's leadership was confident that the new plan was what was needed by the industry they served. It included the creation of new programs, the addition of new member benefits, and aggressive expansion plans.

The association's board of directors and senior staff were surprised at the response from their chapter leadership when the final plan was released. Instead of excitement and enthusiasm for the future, they were met with a tepid and unenthusiastic response. Making the situation more difficult, the national organization's leadership didn't understand why.

As time went on, the national association decided to gather additional feedback from their chapter leaders through a neutral third party. A clear theme emerged when talking with the local stakeholders about the strategic plan. Those leaders did, in fact, agree that the plan was well designed, and that the new programs and services were needed. They simply didn't believe the national organization would implement them effectively. What was the reason for this lack of confidence?

Many chapter leaders indicated that the national organization had consistently failed to meet their expectations related to quality, timeliness, and accuracy of routine communications regarding marketing, dues and invoicing; delivery of existing member services;

and other areas of operations. Simply put, the national organization lacked *Operational Excellence*. This translated into an erosion of confidence in its ability to effectively implement strategy, ultimately resulting in a lack of support and buy-in for the new strategic plan.

As a result, the organization returned to the basics and created a series of operational plans to ensure a foundation of *Operational Excellence* from which to support future strategic initiatives.

This example is a cautionary tale, and it proves an important point: that the best designed strategic plans often fail without a foundation of *Operational Excellence*. Even the best-run associations must continually monitor and improve their operations. This is a primary responsibility of the chief staff officer, who, in turn, empowers other staff to work continuously in the pursuit of *Operational Excellence*.

It is important to underscore that the creation and implementation of operational plans is a staff function. For boards of directors, it should be sufficient to know that operational plans are in place and utilized. Boards of directors should refrain from detailed reviews and/or monitoring operational plans, as micromanaging staff and organizational operations distracts boards from their strategic focus.

Strategic Priority Planning

Just as operational plans are essential to the day-to-day work of an association, it is also critical to develop written plans to guide the implementation of strategic priorities. Strategic priority implementation plans translate strategic initiatives into the steps the association will take to implement them. Typically crafted by staff, they include predefined milestones and measurable outcomes, both of which are linked to deadlines.

The lack of developing a proper plan to implement strategic priorities has resulted in the failure of many strategic initiatives. Creating a plan for implementing strategic priorities builds accountability, transparency, and efficiency, while aligning volunteer, staff, and financial resources.

An example from an anonymous small-staff statewide association illustrates the importance of investing time in building a strategic priority implementation plan.

This association was two years into the implementation of its strategic plan. During its annual meeting, the chief elected officer announced that the organization was embarking on the creation of a new member service, which was part of the association's strategic plan. The board of directors and staff were confident the new service met a member need and would be well received, partly because the identification of this strategic priority had been based on market research and member surveys. However, the response received from members was the opposite. There was a noticeable lack of interest in the service the association would be creating.

The board of directors decided to conduct a phone survey of a portion of the membership to talk with them about their perception of the new service. A list of members reflecting the diversity of the association was created, and as the survey neared the end, a painful truth emerged. The association's leadership was confronted with the reality that during the past several years, there were a number of previous initiatives that had been announced that never materialized, were launched after long delays, or failed to meet member expectations.

In response, the board asked their newly hired chief staff officer to develop a written plan to guide the strategic priority implementation. The board then monitored, at a high level, the major deadlines and other key performance indicators established in the plan as a way of maintaining assurance that priorities were being implemented on time. When the new member service was launched, it was very well received. The association had begun regaining member confidence, while also learning a valuable lesson on the importance of using business plans to ensure strategic success.

Automation

It may seem daunting and time consuming to create operational and strategic priority implementation plans, and even more so to ensure they are used effectively. However, there are an increasing number of technologies and online tools through which plans can easily be developed, modified, and monitored.

These can be particularly useful to leaders in associations that do not already have basic plans in place. It is true that plan creation itself takes a considerable amount of time; however, significant time savings can be realized through automation once the plans are developed. And something else is also true: the more we automate, the less we forget.

There are two primary ways in which automation assists organizational leaders. Automated reminders preceding deadlines and milestones encourage accountability and follow through. And, particularly with operational plans, the automation of routine functions previously physically done by individuals aids in *Operational Excellence* and increases organizational capacity through efficiency. Tasks that many associations currently automate include:

- Invoicing;
- Accounts receivable and past-due reminders;
- Dues billing;
- Membership recruitment messages;
- New member welcome messages;
- Registration solicitations;
- Event and education registration reminders; and
- Participation and donor thank you messages.

Automation doesn't come without risk, though. With increased use, it is possible to forget about some of the tasks that are completed automatically. In the case of communications that are distributed automatically, there is also a risk that the language used becomes outdated. In order to mitigate these risks, it is best to create an automation plan.

An automation plan includes a list of every organizational function that has been automated, as well as the dates or frequency by which they occur. A well-designed automation plan also includes an annual or periodic review so that changes may be made, such as eliminating outdated functions, updating communications text, and adding new automated tasks.

Ensuring a Healthy Organizational Ecosystem

Ensuring *Operational Excellence* also means looking at an organization holistically. In fact, association leaders must routinely evaluate the health of the organization they serve in order to ensure the success of their operational and strategic plans. Often times, institution trumps innovation. Many strategic plans fail due to institutional structure, culture, and processes that have gone unevaluated for too long.

Leaders should think of their associations in the context of an ecosystem. The overall health of an ecosystem is dependent on the interconnectedness of the elements within it. The same is true for an organizational ecosystem.

A good way to understand how to define key elements of an organizational ecosystem is to look to nature. In an aquatic ecosystem, we find water, fish, algae, coral, plankton, and many other essential elements. The presence—and health—of each of these elements is essential for the overall health of the ecosystem. It is relatively easy to create this aquatic list; however, how do we begin to define the key elements in an organizational ecosystem?

Building on the concepts developed in *From Insight to Action: Six New Ways to Think, Lead, and Achieve,* published by Association Management Press, this becomes easy. The authors define eight elements that are essential to organizational health.

1. **Purpose** is the reason for an organization's existence and, despite changes to the external environment or profession or issues facing areas in which the organization operates, purpose represents the one thing that members and stakeholders can never envision changing.

2. **Principles** are beliefs and values that guide an organization's behavior, decisions, and actions.

3. **Potential** is a clear articulation of the future the organization wishes to create. Achievement of the organization's full potential is often expressed in its vision, goals, and aspirational statements. As organizations dedicate themselves to reaching their full potential, they can create positive change in the world.

4. **Processes** are repeatable methods of executing work and making decisions. Leaders function best in organizations that have built processes that result in operational efficiencies and quality outcomes.

5. **Priorities** represent a focused set of initiatives chosen in an operational time frame. Successful organizations select these priorities in light of their Purpose and Principles, while keeping in mind their limited resources of people, time, and money. Priorities are not about rank-ordering a long list; they are about selecting what to do and what not to do.

6. **People** involve the relationships in an organization that are based on mutual respect and trust, and a shared understanding of the roles people play in organizational success. In an association, this includes staff, members, volunteers, and stakeholders; in other organizations, it may be employees and customers or clients, as appropriate to the organization's particular business model.

7. **Praise** represents a genuine, expressed appreciation for the people within an organization as well as individuals served by it. Praise is about celebrating success and valuing the role that people play in achieving success.

8. **Planet** is a clear understanding of how fulfilling Purpose achieves positive change in the world around the organization. It means different things for different organizations and should not be equated solely with environmental sustainability. It is a fundamental awareness that what people and organizations do can have a ripple effect in the communities in which they operate and in the world as a whole.

An organizational assessment based on these eight elements is on page 107. This assessment provides leaders with an easy-to-use tool to evaluate the health of their organization. It also enables leaders to develop a shared understanding of key elements within their organization, and results in a visual tool to guide decisions related to necessary organizational change.

Associations that have used this organizational assessment better understand their health. The assessment creates increased communication among organizational leaders about the foundational elements of the organization, and also results in a shared understanding of areas of *Operational Excellence* as well as areas for growth.

The tool, when used by staff and/or members, also effectively sparks conversation around organizational culture, change, and direction. This all increases the likelihood that an organization will successfully implement strategic priorities and operational tactics in support of those priorities.

Questions to Consider

• Does our association have operational plans in place for key functions?

• Do we develop a plan to guide the implementation of strategic priorities?

• Do we ensure there are sufficient funds budgeted for both operational and strategic priorities?

• What areas of our association's operations can we automate?

• What is the health of our association's ecosystem?

Chapter 5

....

Maintaining Focus

Maintaining Focus is one of the most difficult yet essential things for organizations to do. The most obvious area on which associations need to focus is their mission. And being mission-centric implies that all elements in a strategic plan further the organization's purpose and advance its reason for existing. While this type of focus is absolutely essential, unfortunately it is not enough.

Organizations must also maintain a heightened focus on strategy implementation. It is easy for a board of directors to get caught up in the mechanics and details of an organization, with much of a board's focus drifting inappropriately into operational management and engagement in routine programs and services. This, however, is counterproductive to the board's primary role of governance. In terms of strategic plan implementation, the board's primary role is crafting elements of the plan and selecting priorities. Ideally, this is done collaboratively with senior staff. To maintain focus on its governance role, effective boards delegate to the chief staff officer the responsibility for implementing strategic priorities. In turn, the chief staff officer empowers staff and/or engages member volunteers in the process of implementation.

There are three primary ways in which leaders can ensure proper focus on strategy. First, a limited number of strategic priorities should be selected for implementation at any given time. Second, it is a key responsibility of the board of directors to monitor and benchmark progress against the strategic plan at a high level. And, last, association leaders should exhibit sufficient flexibility to capitalize on unforeseen opportunities or guard against quickly arising threats or changes.

Limited Number of Priorities

In the excitement of developing or revising a strategic plan, an association's board of directors may be tempted to select too many priorities for implementation too quickly. Often, the more an association thinks it does well, the less it does effectively. Implementation of strategic priorities must be balanced with organizational capacity and resources.

Associations should select their priorities by looking through two lenses: fulfilling their core identity and understanding the environment in which the organization exists. Core identity is defined as an organization's mission, vision, and values; and it is supported by its organizational capacity and competency. Environmental scanning is also essential to selecting the right priorities, helping organizational leaders better understand the environment in which they are operating. It provides insight into ongoing changes within the profession or industry the organization serves, and sheds light on macro issues affecting stakeholders. It can also reveal if there should be a particular sense of urgency around any strategic priorities.

The book From Insight to Action: Six New Ways to Think, Lead, and Achieve, published by ASAE's Association Management Press, provides additional guidance for organizations in crafting achievable priorities. It suggests five characteristics that well-designed priorities share:

1. **Focused**: Priorities must be focused on the organization's purpose/mission. This ensures they are aligned with the reason the organization exists and helps ensure a mission-centric strategy.

2. **Fit**: Priorities must fit with the organization's competencies, resources, and principles (values). This ensures that priorities do not exceed organizational capacity.

3. **Flexible**: The expressed ability for organizational leaders to adjust priorities as circumstances evolve, which is explored in greater detail on page 43.

4. **Fact-Based**: Priorities are based on research and data. This helps association leaders ground their decisions in fact rather than opinion.

5. **Feel Right**: The selection of priorities allows for the blending of intuition and data. This is a concept covered in significant detail in the book *From Insight to Action.*

These characteristics provide association leaders with a road map to ensure their strategic priorities are well designed. This can be considered half the battle in maintaining focus. The other half is selecting a limited number of priorities on which to work at any given time. The case study below highlights how one association has used these concepts to maintain strategic focus.

AHRA: The Association for Medical Imaging Management developed a strategic plan that included nearly 40 priorities. Although it was a multi-year plan, the organization initially earmarked nearly 85 percent of the priorities to be implemented during the first year after the plan was finalized. Naturally, this resulted in a lack of focus and a struggle to successfully implement nearly 35 new priorities in a single year.

At the end of the first year, the association's leadership decided to refocus the organization on implementing only three priorities. To do so, they evaluated how the priorities in the existing strategic plan supported the association's core identity, and responded to the environment in which it was operating. Once the priorities were selected, staff developed a plan to implement the priorities and track progress.

According to the organization's staff team, the selection of a limited number of priorities through these lenses provided the organization with a crystal-clear focus and also aided in aligning the organization's resources in the most effective way to implement its strategic plan. The implementation plan built by staff, combined with updates presented at every board of directors meeting, provided the board with assurance that progress was being made and the priorities were being accomplished. Combined, the implementation plan and board updates also helped the board of directors to focus its time during meetings on the strategy and direction of the organization.

This example highlights the power of a board of directors and staff working collaboratively to successfully focus an association on strategy implementation.

The American Association for Adult and Continuing Education (AAACE) also strengthened its ability to implement its strategic plan by narrowing its focus to a limited number of priorities each year. The association had developed a six-page strategic plan with few clear priorities assigned to any given year. This resulted in a challenge for the organization's member volunteers and staff who were attempting to implement a large number of priorities at the same time and dramatically slowed implementation of the entire strategic plan.

After several years, the association developed a new, one-page strategic plan and clearly identified five goals to be implemented during its first year. The shorter strategic plan, combined with regular progress updates from staff, also assisted the board of directors in focusing on strategy and governance during its meetings, elevating the quality of conversation and engagement of board members. This focus also increased the pace of change within the organization. This built significant momentum within the organization so that when their goals were accomplished at the end of the first year of their new strategic plan, the organization selected another limited number on which to focus during the following year. In this way, AAACE was able to maintain focus on implementing its entire strategic plan.

As is evident from both AHRA and AAACE, each association must carefully consider how many priorities it can implement in a single year. While there is no single number that will fit every organization, one thing is consistently true: Less is more.

Monitoring Progress

A board of directors must routinely monitor and evaluate progress to ensure continual focus on implementation of a strategic plan. Traditionally, this has been done by providing reports, whether written or verbal. While this approach can be effective, it can also create a situation in which board members become too focused on minutia, and lose focus on the big picture. Therefore, some innovative associations are developing new tools to help their boards maintain focus and monitor strategic progress.

The use of dashboard reporting has become a best practice in the nonprofit sector. With dashboard reporting, progress is evaluated not by lengthy reports, but by looking at a limited number of key performance indicators on a continual basis, often in the form of graphs and charts. This provides a quick way to evaluate various areas of the association's operations.

While dashboards have been primarily used to report operational metrics, some associations are adapting them to indicate progress on strategic priorities as well. The utility of these strategic dashboard reports, not surprisingly, flows from two other concepts discussed previously in this book: simplicity and visual communication.

The Construction Specifications Institute (CSI) leveraged the dashboard concept by creating a simple tool to give its board of directors a quick and visual way to gauge progress on the implementation of strategic initiatives. The association's staff developed a report in which each strategic initiative is listed alongside a traffic light color as a visual indication of its current status. The traffic light is green if the priority is completed or progressing according to schedule, yellow if it is somewhat complete or slightly behind schedule, or red if there is no progress or if it is substantially behind established implementation benchmarks.

Furthermore, this dashboard was created during a chief staff officer transition, in which CSI also changed how its board and staff collaborate. They adopted the Policy Governance® Model, which is a comprehensive governance system developed by Dr. John Carver. This affected every aspect of how the organization is led, and the use of a strong visual aided them greatly during this transition.

Example of a Strategic Priority Implementation Dashboard

Status	Definition of Status
R Y **G**	**[Green]** Priority is completed or is progressing according to schedule
R **Y** G	**[Yellow]** Priority is somewhat complete, or slightly behind schedule
R Y G	**[Red]** There is no progress being made on the priority, or it is substantially behind established implementation benchmarks

Report on each strategic priority separately in the grid below, filling in green, yellow, or red circles for each benchmark to visually indicate progress in Status column.

Strategic Priority #1:

Status	Established measurable benchmarks	Comments on current progress
R Y G	1.	
R Y G	2.	
R Y G	3.	

Strategic Priority #2:

Status	Established measurable benchmarks	Comments on current progress
R Y G	1.	
R Y G	2.	
R Y G	3.	

Utilizing this dashboard has helped transition the board of directors from focusing on tactics to spending more time discussing the organization's strategic direction, as well as the end results desired, and the overall progress in strategic plan implementation. Additionally, failure to meet a measure of success triggers a positive, results-oriented discussion about what needs to be done, about whether the objective is still important (or takes priority over other objectives), and about its relative importance given finite resources. This approach reduces the likelihood board members will micromanage staff, and also has the added benefit of fostering an environment in which the board as a whole offers insight and feedback regarding strategy. This helps the organization to more easily navigate changes in the marketplace it serves.

This example from CSI underscores the importance of dashboard reporting when it comes to maintaining focus on strategic priorities, and how using simple, visual dashboard reports can be a powerful strategic tool.

Nonprofit organizations are increasingly using dashboard reporting with strong visual elements to communicate progress on strategic initiatives. From literally placing a traffic light graphic next to each priority on a report, to the use of more formal systems, the goal is always the same: to quickly and effectively help organizational leaders understand the current state of strategic progress at a particular point in time.

A simplified version of dashboard reporting using traffic light graphics follows.

Strategic Priority Progress Traffic Light Dashboard

The color of the traffic light next to a strategic priority indicates the current status of the priority. The light is green if the priority is completed or is progressing according to schedule. It is yellow if the priority is somewhat complete, or slightly behind schedule. The light is red if there is no progress being made on the priority, or if it is substantially behind established implementation benchmarks.

Status	Strategic Priority
Ⓡ Ⓨ Ⓖ	_____
Ⓡ Ⓨ Ⓖ	_____
Ⓡ Ⓨ Ⓖ	_____

Understanding the Implementation Timeline

The implementation of every strategic priority has several key deadlines. A shared awareness of these deadlines between staff and board is critical for transparency and accountability. Traditionally, these benchmarks have been communicated by association staff to boards of directors through written reports, or perhaps spreadsheets. The Building Owners and Managers Association of Georgia developed a different approach for sharing key strategic deadlines with its board of directors. It developed a visual timeline which is shown below.

STRATEGIC GOALS FOR THE YEAR

Goal 1: **Create a Real Estate Summit**

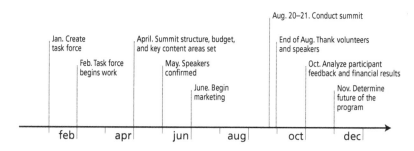

Goal 2: **Enhance New Member Engagement**

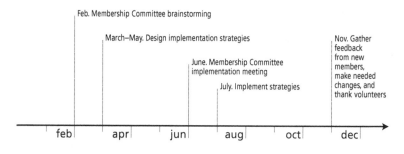

Source: BOMA Georgia. Reprinted with permission.

The timeline was developed to provide the board of directors with a big-picture overview of benchmarks that are related to strategic priorities.

Use of this visual timeline has resulted in increased transparency and an increase in member understanding of the length of time for implementing strategic priorities. Shared awareness of key milestones also creates accountability for on-time implementation of the steps needed to successfully complete a priority. The tool has also aided the board of directors in focusing its attention on the current and future status of strategic priorities, preventing it from looking backward, and helping the association monitor progress.

Flexibility

The best ideas don't always emerge according to a strategic planning timeline. Sometimes thoughts on improving upon an idea emerge during implementation, or member needs may change quickly due to unforeseen circumstances. And disruptive change may occur at any time. Therefore, organizational leaders need to remain flexible when implementing strategic priorities.

However, in nonprofit organizations there is no shortage of ideas. In fact, if there is one thing an association always has more of than members, it is ideas. All members have at least a few ideas that they would like to see implemented by the association. Therefore, there is a responsibility for the board of directors to determine which strategic ideas are implemented, and which are not. Doing so is fraught with potential conflict.

The Georgia Society of Association Executives promotes a tool, beginning on page 101, which helps organizational leaders evaluate ideas as they emerge throughout the year. Association leaders ask a series of questions based on three areas:

1. **Vision:** How does the program or service support the association's core purpose (mission, vision, values)?

2. **Resources:** Does the association have the financial and human capital resources to implement the program or service?

3. **Consequences:** What consequences may occur if the idea is approved or denied?

This model provides an objective process for evaluating new ideas as they emerge throughout the year. The process diminishes the likelihood of approving new programs or services that detract from established strategic priorities or overcommitting an organization's resources. It also reduces the likelihood that new programs or services are approved based on opinion, or on who presents them.

A Georgia-based trade association used this process to consider the creation of a new young professionals shared interest group for its membership. The idea was presented to the chief staff officer by a group of young professionals near the middle of the year, at which time several other strategic priorities were in various stages of implementation. Since the idea fit well into the existing strategic plan, it was forwarded to the board of directors for further consideration.

The board evaluated the proposed program's fit in terms of vision, resources, and consequences, as outlined in the assessment. In the end, the board decided that creating a young professionals shared interest group would fit nicely within the strategic direction of the organization—but that it also didn't have capacity to do so at that time.

When they reported back to the group of young professionals who had initially presented the idea, the group was disappointed but not disenfranchised. The group had read and understood the process the board used in evaluating their proposal. This eliminated potential accusations of personal bias and anchored the decision on an objective and transparent process.

Because the idea did fit within the strategic direction of the association, it was also immediately added to the strategic plan. Six months later, when the board of directors was selecting a limited number of priorities to implement for the following year, the creation of a young professionals shared interest group was selected as a top priority.

Questions to Consider

- Are our strategic priorities in support of our organization's core identity (mission, vision, and values) and responsive to the environment in which we are operating?

- In what way(s) can we provide the board of directors with a visual tool to monitor strategic progress?

- How can we develop a shared understanding of the timeline for implementing strategic priorities?

- In what ways does our organization exhibit flexibility if circumstances change while implementing strategic priorities?

- Do we have an objective, written process for vetting new ideas that emerge throughout the year?

Chapter 6

Absolute Alignment

Once strategic priorities are selected, many association leaders think first about how to align the priorities with the organization's budget. While it is obviously necessary to ensure adequate financial resources for the implementation of strategic plans, it may be less obvious that alignment of human resources is even more critical.

The nonprofit sector is rich with mission-driven volunteers and professional staff passionate about making a difference. This creates an abundance of individuals who are eager to engage in work that is core to an association's purpose. But how do the best organizations blend the technical expertise of association staff with the industry and professional knowledge of members and volunteers? Savvy associations largely delegate this responsibility to their chief staff officer, who is responsible for aligning the workforce with the organization's needs. There are two pillars that guide the decisions on how to do so: role clarity and empowerment.

Role Clarity

Misunderstanding regarding the roles and responsibilities of members and staff is one of the major sources of conflict in nonprofit organizations. As a result, establishing clearly defined roles is an essential step in successfully implementing organizational strategy.

While many organizations create charges—a written bullet point list of what a group is responsible for doing—to guide committee and task force work, this is often not enough. Member volunteers, excited to serve the organization may, at times, venture outside the bounds of their charges and engage in work assigned to staff. It is easy to see how this happens. If the written charges neglect to mention key aspects of a project's work, members may assume they should complete those tasks. The following examples exemplify this dilemma.

A statewide organization was planning a major fundraising event. It had assembled a committee of members to assist in selling sponsorships, generating auction donations, and encouraging attendance through word-of-mouth marketing. At one of the committee's meetings, a member presented a venue contract for the group to consider. This member had taken it upon himself to negotiate an event venue through a professional relationship, without consulting the staff or the committee chair. Needless to say, the member's enthusiasm quickly changed to embarrassment and confusion when he was told that staff had already signed a contract for the event space. This misunderstanding could have been easily avoided.

To reduce misunderstandings such as this, a written list of responsibilities for staff and other stakeholder groups should be developed when they engage with committees or other member work groups. This list should be made available to all member volunteers, in addition to an outline of the traditional committee/task force charges.

Building on the previous example, the following charges could have been developed to clarify the role of members and staff in producing the fundraising event:

Fundraising Event Committee Charges
- Sell sponsorships
- Generate silent auction donations
- Encourage friends and colleagues to attend the event through word-of-mouth marketing

Staff Charges
- Develop sponsorship packages
- Secure the event venue
- Create and implement a marketing plan, beyond word-of-mouth communications
- Manage the financial and logistical operations of the event

These charges could be approved by the board of directors or executive committee. They could then be listed on every agenda for the fundraising event committee, which would reinforce role clarity among members and staff. This approach would greatly reduce the potential for ambiguity of responsibilities and conflict among people.

Developing a written list of responsibilities for members and staff sounds easy, but there is still the matter of deciding who should do what. To do so, organizational leaders must evaluate the unique knowledge, skills, and relationships that members and staff each bring to an organization, and then align the work of the organization accordingly.

- **Knowledge:** What unique expertise is required?

- **Skills:** What skill sets will aid in the project?

- **Relationships:** What professional relationships will aid in the implementation?

Evaluating these three areas provides an objective framework through which association leaders can align their workforce, both member and staff, to accomplish their organization's goals. The framework provides consistency, and removes subjectivity and emotion from the decision-making process. And more importantly, it puts individuals in the roles in which they are best equipped for success.

Nardone Consulting Group, Inc., an Atlanta-based association management company, has effectively used this framework with its clients. With one association in particular, there had been a misunderstanding between members and staff about who was responsible for key aspects of an annual networking event. Over the course of several years, members increasingly took on responsibilities for which staff had a greater expertise. This created confusion among members and staff, lack of consistency in event planning from year to year, and, surprisingly, it actually increased the amount of time required by staff to produce the event.

To create a shared understanding of who should be responsible for which aspects of the project, a written list of the key tasks necessary to produce the event was created. Then, the board of directors discussed what knowledge, skills, and relationships were necessary to best accomplish each task. Finally, the group determined if members or staff should be responsible for accomplishing each task based solely on who had the necessary knowledge, skills, and relationships.

This exercise was a turning point for the association's leadership. It helped them to better understand the unique roles members and staff play in a nonprofit organization. The role clarity also resulted in increased communication, transparency, and efficiency. And it has further strengthened the member–staff relationship.

A role-clarity grid designed to assist associations in this process is on page 99.

While it is not necessary for every organization to formally go through a process like this, this case study underscores the need for written, clearly defined roles among members and staff. And it highlights the positive change that occurs when such role clarity is produced.

Conflict can also occur between member groups. One of the most common sources of member-to-member conflict is between those serving on a board of directors and those who serve on a subset of the board, the executive committee. Without role clarity and transparency between these groups, conflict arises. This lack of clarity and transparency can create a situation in which the executive committee is perceived as a mysterious group within the board of directors, making decisions that the board will simply rubber stamp. While some nonprofit organizations have discontinued the use of executive committees, in many organizations they have an important, strategic role to play.

Ideally, an executive committee is the servant of the board. While it may make necessary decisions in between board meetings, its more central role should be in equipping the board with the tools it needs to make strategic decisions. It may also take a more granular look at some issues so that the full board can more easily maintain its strategic focus.

There are three key aspects of an executive committee functioning as a servant of the board of directors: strategy, research, and transparency.

Board of directors meetings should largely focus on the ongoing and future strategy of the organization. Each board meeting should include discussion topics that support current strategic priorities and/or other elements of the strategic plan. But by whom should the discussion topics be decided? Identifying and selecting strategic discussion topics can be a natural role of the executive committee.

Next, once strategic discussion topics are selected, there may be a need for additional research so that the board of directors has a common and current knowledge base from which to discuss. Identifying research needs and ensuring the board of directors has sufficient background information to make informed decisions is another good role for an executive committee that is operating as the servant of the board.

Finally, it is very important for an executive committee to ensure that its operations are transparent to the board. Sharing executive committee minutes with the full board of directors and annually discussing the group's role in governance are two ways to increase transparency and remove the perception of mystery from the executive committee.

A sample executive committee orientation is on page 95. The orientation is designed to frame the executive committee as the servant of the board of directors.

Additionally, beyond the executive committee, failure to properly train all new committee and task force leaders can also sow the seeds of potential conflict. Members have a natural desire to serve nonprofit organizations they care about. However, members often lack formal training in how to properly and effectively serve in a leadership capacity. In fact, for many members, an opportunity to serve as a committee leader may be the first formal leadership they have had. A sample committee chair orientation process is on page 89. It is designed to assist association leaders in providing sound, consistent training for committee leadership.

Empower Others

Once the expected roles among members and staff have been clearly defined, individuals assigned with carrying out responsibilities on behalf of the association must be empowered to accomplish their tasks. This is another common pitfall for associations. It is easy for a board of directors to tell a member work group not just what to do but also how to do it. And it may be tempting for chief staff officers to over-direct the work of their staff team, diminishing creativity, enthusiasm, and buy-in. How, then, should work be directed?

Generally speaking, association leaders should ask that member and staff work be completed according to three guidelines:

1. **Efficient:** Is the work being produced with respect to the association's budget and timeline?

2. **Effective**: Is the work produced meeting, or exceeding, predefined benchmarks of quality?

3. **Ethical**: Is the means by which the work is done honest and ethical?

In terms of strategic planning, the primary responsibility of the board of directors must be creating vision, setting strategy, and defining priorities. The board must also be cautious to ensure it doesn't extend itself into the role of implementation. Successful implementation of strategic plans demands empowerment within all levels of the organization. The board is empowered to dream, while committees, staff, and members are empowered to do. This results in a culture of inclusion, creativity, and engagement and ensures strategic priorities are achieved.

Mind Redesign Consulting has worked extensively in assisting nonprofit organizations to achieve role clarity. A case study of a particular organization with which the consulting firm has worked highlights how role clarity and empowerment improve both operational and strategic effectiveness.

The company was engaged with a 501(c)(3) community-based organization in which two of its founding members were heavily involved in the organization's operations, many years after it was founded. Both individuals announced their intention to depart the organization within the next five years. As a result, the board of directors began to think more critically about succession planning, and, as part of that conversation, the board realized there was a lack of consensus about the future roles of senior staff and board members. Throughout the years, staff had assumed a greater role not just of operations, but of governance as well. This resulted in ambiguity among several board members as to their proper role in serving the organization.

To regain clarity, a consultant led the group through a process of creating written guidelines for board and staff involvement in strategic planning, programming, governance, and operations of the organization. The written guidelines empowered both members and staff to serve the organization *efficiently, effectively,* and *ethically,* within the parameters created. This also helped the organization better focus their member and staff resources; more closely align the work of its volunteers and staff with the organization's mission; and establish an understanding of the roles individuals played in serving the nonprofit.

This example also reinforces the guiding philosophy that the board of directors governs an organization, while the staff manages it. Ideally, members and staff collaborate in governance in terms of crafting strategy and setting priorities. This is because members and staff have complementary perspectives that, when combined, result in better decisions being made for the organization they serve.

Questions to Consider

- What areas of our organization would benefit from additional role clarity?

- Do our committees, task forces, and other work groups have a written list of responsibilities? Do staff and other stakeholder groups with whom those groups work also have a written list of responsibilities?

- In what ways can our executive committee be more of a servant to the board of directors?

- How can we more effectively empower others in implementing our strategic priorities?

Chapter 7

Iterative Innovation

There is much associations can learn from the technology sector. The seemingly exponential advancement in technology is rapidly changing people's lives, both personally and professionally. And the ubiquitous reach of the internet is integrating life and data, as well as making us more reliant on technology. One of the key philosophies driving this growth relates to how technology companies design, build, and sell their products and services.

Prototyping and beta-testing are cornerstones of technology development. TechTarget defines prototyping as, "A systems development method in which a prototype (an early approximation of a final system or product) is built, tested, and then reworked as necessary until an acceptable prototype is finally achieved from which the complete system or product can now be developed. It is an iterative, trial-and-error process that takes place between the developers and the users."

There is much that associations can learn from this definition. In particular, three components of the definition can guide the use of prototyping in the nonprofit sector:

- **Iterative process:** Initial assumptions and research are tested through an initial prototype and then retested through subsequent versions of the product or service.

- **Opportunity for learning:** Each iteration of the product or service allows members and staff to learn, both from objective data and observations as well as the subjective perspective of users and developers.

- **Feedback between developers and users**: Incorporating an opportunity for feedback from members and others who use the product or service increases communication, fosters engagement, and aids the learning process.

While not every strategic priority is ripe for prototyping, the priorities that are share some common characteristics:

- The program or service can be easily divided into segments that stand alone, or future iterations of the entire program or service can be easily modified;

- There is a sense of urgency in meeting a need through the development of the strategic priority; and

- Learning from the initial launch of the program or service will significantly influence its future development and refinement.

There are many benefits to the use of prototyping when launching a strategic plan initiative, including: greatly increased speed to market; testing of the validity of initial assumptions; gauging the long-term relevance of the initiative; building in opportunities for continual improvement; creating an opportunity for greater integration of intuition throughout the process; increasing stakeholder engagement through feedback; and harnessing the collective wisdom of staff, association leaders, members, and ultimately of all end users of the product or service.

There are three prerequisites that must be in place before an association uses iterative innovation. First, there must be no ambiguity in the roles that members and staff will play during the prototyping process. Second, association leaders, and boards collectively, need to increase their comfort with risk taking. And third, boards of directors and staff must see failure as positive, and as an opportunity for learning and growth, since it informs future iterations of strategic initiatives.

BOMI International, a 501(c)(3) adult education organization, has frequently used prototyping. Most recently, BOMI used this model in developing a new High Performance designation program for real estate professionals. After conducting significant research on high performance buildings, BOMI convened a group of subjected matter experts, who, along with staff, developed a vision for the program.

The initial design included the creation of three 24-hour classes, which validated learning through scenario-based examination. A full prototype of each class was developed and then taught as a pilot class in three separate markets throughout the United States. Based on student feedback, significant changes were needed to all three prototype courses.

Initially, BOMI anticipated finalizing development of all three courses on a parallel track, leading to a simultaneous release of the classes and full launch of the program. However, due to the magnitude of the project and student feedback, the organization shifted its approach to an *Iterative Innovation* model, developing and launching each course separately.

This change in development strategy provided a variety of benefits to the organization. It increased learning from student and instructor feedback through each course pilot and launch, which better informed development of future classes. It spread the financial cost of development over a longer period of time, and derived revenue from courses as they were launched, while also testing new strategies in adult learning. And finally, it engaged a team of stakeholder volunteers and staff to ensure consistency of quality and cohesiveness of content across the three courses.

BOMI's use of *Iterative Innovation* resulted in a three-course designation that was more responsive to student feedback than developing the courses simultaneously ever could have been. The launch of each individual course served as a focus group, and the lessons learned were used to make subsequent courses more engaging and relevant.

Steps in Using Iterative Innovation
What does the *Iterative Innovation* process look like? Adapted from prototyping, the following steps outline the process associations can use:

1. Select a strategic priority and define key performance indicators, milestones, budget, and a timeline.

2. Clearly define the roles and responsibilities volunteers and staff will have throughout the process.

3. Create a preliminary design of the program or service.

4. Build the program or service based on step three (realizing that at this stage it may not include all of the features envisioned in the final version).

5. Launch the program or service.

6. Compare the results against initial expectations from step one and through feedback from those using the product or service.

7. Modify the initial program or service based on what was learned, and create a revised, improved version.

8. Repeat the previous steps as many times as necessary until the final product or service meets member and stakeholder expectations.

9. Seek feedback continually to ensure the ongoing relevance of the program or service.

The *Iterative Innovation* model has the power to transform associations. It increases the speed of delivery of new programs and services, creates flexibility, and integrates continual learning. And it aids organizational leaders in moving beyond strategic planning to effectively implement new ideas.

The National Art Education Association (NAEA) embraces *Iterative Innovation*. In fact, the association has used the concept for years as it implements strategic priorities. Examining how NAEA applied *Iterative Innovation* to developing its School for Art Leaders program highlights the utility and value of applying this concept in a nonprofit organization.

The association's strategic plan called for the development of a new comprehensive leadership training program for art educators, who are teaching kindergarten through college. NAEA assembled a task force of members and staff who researched leadership competencies through the lens of art educators. The group then built a framework that integrated the leadership competencies with activities and exercises they hoped would reinforce their development among participants.

Rather than launching the full program at the conclusion of their research, NAEA decided to invite members to participate in individual modules of the program. More than 150 members engaged in at least one of the modules and provided feedback on their experience. This provided NAEA with a wide range of member perspectives on how to strengthen the program. Patterns identified through this feedback enabled staff to further refine the program and assemble it into a comprehensive leadership program.

With the full launch of the School for Art Leaders the following year, a cohort of 25 individuals was selected through an application process to go through a 7-month leadership development program together. However, the launch of the program was not the end of the association's iterative approach to its development. In conjunction with the first-year program, the association launched a longitudinal study to understand the program's long-term impact on participants. This, combined with feedback from each subsequent class of participants, allows NAEA to continually evolve the program to meet participant needs and expectations, as well as address changes in best practices and accountability in education and academic environments.

The results of the of this *Iterative Innovation* approach to developing the leadership school have been tremendous. Qualitatively and quantitatively, participants have grown as leaders, which has affected their approach to art education and, in turn, positively influenced the lives of thousands of students. Furthermore, demand for participating in the program has exceeded expectations. It has consistently grown each year, most recently with more than triple the number of individuals applying to participate in the program than spots available for the year.

This use of *Iterative Innovation* is not an isolated case for NAEA. The association's chief staff officer and board have integrated the approach into the development of most new strategic initiatives and have used it to continually improve the association's operations as well. It has helped the organization become more nimble and operate in a more entrepreneurial fashion. According to the association's chief staff officer, it has positively affected the mindset of the NAEA's staff and board of directors, encouraging them to embrace flexibility and welcome new ideas. And it has helped the organization's leadership embrace change and continual learning when implementing strategic priorities. They now realize that if there is failure, it is not negative. Rather, it is an opportunity, another step in iteration from which to learn and grow.

The examples from BOMI and NAEA highlight the value and benefits of using *Iterative Innovation* when implementing strategic plan priorities.

Questions to Consider

- Which of our strategic priorities could be successfully implemented though *Iterative Innovation?*

- How would the use of *Iterative Innovation* help us better serve others?

- Do we have an established process for generating feedback through the launch of a new strategic priority?

Chapter 8

. . . .

Systematic Sunsetting

Understanding organizational capacity is just as important as ensuring organizational clarity. Even the best strategic plans can fail due to a lack of capacity. It is easy to underestimate the time, money, or other resources needed to launch a new initiative. It is also easy for associations to erode their ability to achieve strategic priorities over time because they neglect to discontinue programs or services that have outlasted their purpose.

Association boards of directors must become masters at evaluating and discontinuing initiatives, particularly those that no longer meet member or stakeholder needs, achieve essential benchmarks, or align with the organization's strategy. Associations that systematically sunset underperforming or misaligned programs retain a greater organizational capacity for change, by saving staff and volunteer time and financial resources. When redeployed intentionally, this capacity can assist organizations in achieving a higher level of focus on issues of current strategic importance.

One of the best ways to achieve this is to create a plan to review the association's portfolio of programs and services on a regular basis. To review an association's entire array of programs and services at a single time can often prove to be too large and complex of a task. To alleviate this feeling and streamline the process, organizations can create an ongoing review process that examines certain areas of programs and services each year. Here is a sample review schedule:

- Year 1: Education
- Year 2: Events
- Year 3: Advocacy
- Year 4: Other programs and services
- Then repeat the process starting at year 1 again.

Creating a predetermined schedule, in whatever timeline is best for the organization, provides a variety of benefits. It removes the perception of hidden motivations in proposing a review of existing programs, since the association is simply following an established schedule. It assists boards of directors in fulfilling their responsibility to ensure the effective use of organizational capacity. And, of course, this *Systematic Sunsetting* provides increased capacity for the association to implement its strategic plan.

How should association leaders best accomplish this systematic review of their portfolio of programs and services? It is easy for boards of directors to drown in details when discussing the discontinuation of programs or services. It is also possible for board members to allow personal opinion to guide their thoughts. Therefore, a simple, objective process is necessary.

Building on the concepts of simplicity and visualization explained earlier in this book, the following process is designed to assist a board of directors in making the difficult decision of which programs or services to sunset.

Association leaders can create a program grid by first listing each program on a separate line. Then complete the following steps individually for each program:

1. Evaluate each program's fit with the mission of the organization.

2. Calculate the increase/decrease in participation during the last five years.

3. Calculate average net income during the last five years.

4. Estimate the amount of staff time required to produce the program.

5. Estimate the amount of member time required to produce the program.

6. Evaluate the Return on Experience, which is based on feedback from participant surveys.

Using the worksheet on page 106 to enter symbols for the answers to each of these questions, an association may end up with a grid that looks like the one below.

	Mission	Enroll	Net Inc	Time-S	Time-M	ROE
Program #1	Yes	D	$$$	M	L	H
Program #2	Yes	DD	$$	L	H	H
Program #3	Yes	D	$$	M	H	H
Program #4	Yes	DD	$$	H	H	H
Program #5	No	DD	– – –	L	L	L
Program #6	Yes	S	$	L	L	L
Program #7	No	S	–	L	L	L
Program #8	Yes	S	$	L	M	L
Program #9	Yes	GG	$	M	M	M
Program #10	Yes	S	–	M	M	M
Program #11	Yes	GG	–	M	M	M
Program #12	Yes	GG	–	M	M	M
Program #13	Yes	G	$	L	M	L
Program #14	Yes	DD	– –	M	M	M

Using this program grid, an organization's leadership will be more easily able to identify potential programs to sunset or reinvent, without getting caught up in the details of extensive financial reports and other data. In fact, the results included in this grid reveal some interesting points of consideration for this hypothetical association's leadership.

The organization's most profitable programs are experiencing a decrease in enrollment, while its least profitable programs are gaining participation. There are two existing programs that fall outside of the association's mission, and are potentially ripe for sunsetting. An effective board of directors will look even deeper, asking itself what other insights may be drawn from this grid and discussed.

This model is presented as a visual tool to assist association leadership in better understanding and evaluating their programs and services, and to potentially sunset programs. There is, of course, no singular model that will work best for all organizations. It is also important to realize that the responsibility for evaluating and sunsetting programs varies in organizations based on their size and culture. While, of course, the board of directors is ultimately responsible for setting the strategic direction of an organization, the sunsetting process may be conducted by staff, the board of directors, or a staff-member work group. In a large organization with a substantial number of programs and services, the review process may be a staff function, which concludes with high-level recommendations for changes being presented to the board of directors.

Another, more detailed model is presented in the book *Focus on What Matters: A 3-Step Workbook for Selecting and Sunsetting Association Programs, Products, and Services,* published by ASAE's Association Management Press. It provides a comprehensive, data-driven process for evaluating and sunsetting programs and services.

Regardless of the model used, the most critical thing for associations is to have a plan in place and to use it systematically. This point is illustrated by AMC Source. The association management company secured an association as a new client. Recognizing that the association had limited resources and capacity, as many nonprofits do, AMC Source staff led the organization through a review of its programs and services, and then institutionalized the review process as an annual activity. As a result, each year, the board of directors and staff listed all of the organization's programs, services, and member benefits on a matrix and evaluated what was relevant and what needed to be sunsetted.

The annual review process inspired the association's leadership to continually and critically evaluate not just what the organization offers members, but to evaluate its entire value proposition as well. Through the annual review process, it discontinued several services and repositioned the timing and location of others. Capacity generated by discontinuing programs and services was then used to implement the association's new strategic priorities.

The impact of this process was immediate and profound. Within two years of instituting *Systematic Sunsetting*, the association doubled membership, tripled member participation, and quadrupled its net assets.

Questions to Consider

- When was the last time we discontinued a program or service?

- In what ways would *Systematic Sunsetting* of programs and services increase our organizational effectiveness?

- How can *Systematic Sunsetting* create more capacity for implementing strategic priorities?

- Do we have an established, ongoing timeline for the consideration of *Systematic Sunsetting?*

- What and how should we communicate with stakeholders when a program has been selected for sunsetting?

Chapter 9

Strategy-Driven Culture

Strategic planning must evolve from an annual to an ongoing experience. In response to a rapidly changing environment and the increasing pace of change, boards of directors must operate like think tanks. This includes examining macro trends in the environment and micro shifts in the profession or industry they serve. They must set the strategic course for the organization, not just on an annual basis, but continually. Therefore, organizational strategy—and awareness—must be integrated into every facet of the organization.

There are three primary components necessary to building a strategy-driven culture: redefining success, continuously learning, and celebrating success.

Redefining Success

What is the definition of success for an association? And how is success best measured? The answers to these questions have a tremendous impact not just on the perception of success, but also on the allocation of resources, the focus of an organization, and, ultimately what it accomplishes over time.

Traditionally, boards of directors have either explicitly, or implicitly through aggressive monitoring, defined an association's success in terms of membership growth, event attendance, educational enrollment, and similar aspects of an association's operations.

As a result, many associations focus on chasing operational metrics, rather than on implementing and evaluating strategy. The result is that organizational change is often based on responding to shifts in tactical metrics, rather than on establishing and implementing a consistent and focused organizational strategy. Organizations often do this because their definition of success is incomplete.

Associations must largely define success as accomplishing organizational strategy. In a strategy-driven culture, organizations define success as accomplishing a limited number of strategic priorities in any given year. They know that with the right strategy, operational metrics should trend upward over time, as a byproduct of implementing strategic priorities.

In this instance, a board of directors defines success, in writing and at the start of the year, as implementing a limited number of strategic priorities that year. Member and staff time is then allocated accordingly. And for staff, performance review and compensation structures put increased weight on strategic accomplishments.

This is not to say that operations are not important. This approach assumes *Operational Excellence* is being maintained, and it relies on the philosophy that organizations get more of what they measure. In this case, measuring and motivating completion of strategic priorities aids in building a strategy-driven culture.

The Indiana Music Education Association has embraced the concept of defining success as implementing strategic priorities. Doing so transitioned the board of directors away from an operational focus, and into a board that focuses on governance and setting organizational strategy. The change also led to some significant developments for the association.

The board's increased level of strategic conversations inspired them to change the organization's name from the Indiana Music Educators Association to the Indiana Music Education Association, reflecting the impact the association has not just on teachers, but also on students. This resulted in changes to the association's portfolio of programs and services so that their impact on student performance could clearly be seen. It also helped the board to more clearly see the association's role in advocating for the profession to stakeholders throughout the state.

And, as is often the case, defining success as implementing strategic priorities also created another tangible byproduct: growth in operational metrics. Over the course of four years, the association grew annual revenue by 10 percent and increased attendance in professional development programs by nearly 50 percent.

Continuously Learning

Member preferences evolve, stakeholder needs shift, and circumstances change. Therefore, association leaders must engage in continuous learning about the marketplace in which they operate. One should not simply create a multi-year strategic plan, and then follow it as a roadmap without questioning unforeseen turns as they occur. Association leaders must also continually learn by asking questions, observing changes, and identifying patterns—even after a plan has been created.

Many associations rely on member and nonmember surveys to do this. However, this is not enough. There are many other ways leaders can gain insight that is often not found in routine surveys.

A state-based individual membership organization developed a program modeled after the secret shopper concept, to continually learn about and improve its events. Prior to key events, the association staff contacts a select number of new members, or others who are attending for the first time, and asks if they will share feedback based on their experience. Patterns will often emerge from this feedback, revealing opportunities for improvement, and helping association leaders gain perspective. An additional benefit of seeking this type of feedback is increased engagement from individuals participating in the program, simply by giving them an opportunity to provide it.

Other associations keep logs of unsolicited feedback, tracking suggestions, compliments, and complaints from members received via phone, email, or in person. These logs help association leaders to quickly identify changes needed in operations to better serve members, while also revealing patterns in member needs and wants. These revelations can have profound implications in identifying new ways to strategically meet and exceed member expectations.

Organizational leaders may also quickly identify trends and patterns through monitoring member and stakeholder use of social media. This can be very useful in better understanding current and emerging trends affecting the profession or industry an association serves. Insight gained can be used to better craft and implement strategic priorities to ensure they are meeting current and future needs.

There is also an important role for the board of directors to play in continuous learning. Board agendas should be crafted to focus significant time on strategic conversations related to priorities in the organization's strategic plan. The book *The Will to Govern Well*, published by Association Management Press, provides insight in how to craft discussions around issues of strategic importance, which the authors refer to as "mega-issues."

Incorporating governance strategies from *The Will to Govern Well* routinely at board meetings ensures a board of directors is focused on its governance role, while remaining in a state of continuous learning. As a result, conversations around strategy at board meetings will increasingly result in additional clarity, shared understanding, prioritization, and/or understanding related to the strategic direction of the organization.

Celebrating Success

At its base, an association is about people. It is created to provide a public good, and an opportunity for people to collaborate in making a positive difference in the world around them.

It takes a tremendous amount of effort from people to create and successfully implement a strategic plan. Far too often, though, the people who engage in the strategic work of an organization are not recognized for their contributions. While it is important for an association to celebrate accomplishing its strategic priorities, it is even more important to celebrate individual contributions.

A truly strategic culture celebrates success by recognizing those who made that success possible. It is easy to take for granted that members are willing and excited to serve an association. It is also easy to forget that the time they invest is a choice, and they could have easily decided to spend their time differently.

Fortunately, there is a simple and effective way to build a continuously learning environment and also ensure those who contribute to the implementation of strategic priorities are thanked and appreciated. There should be two tactics which accompany the end of every strategic priority. First, those involved should discuss and document what was learned and what can be improved. Second, the individuals who contributed to the process should be recognized and thanked.

Including these two simple, yet important, tactics will support a culture of continual learning, and ensure that organizational leaders never forget to thank those who contributed to the success.

Questions to Consider

• How do we define organizational success?

• How does our definition of success support or detract from implementing strategic initiatives?

• In what ways, beyond surveys, do we identify patterns and gain new insight?

• How can we more effectively and routinely thank those who engage in implementing strategic priorities?

RESOURCES

The tips, tools, and techniques in this section are designed to assist organizations in all stages of their strategic planning and implementation efforts. It is often challenging for organizational leaders to translate concepts into realty. As a result, these tools are included to provide a variety of resources to assist in moving beyond strategic planning to *Strategic Integration*.

False Starts:
13 Ways to Mess Up Strategic Planning

Boards of directors can feel uncomfortable by strategic thinking, finding it easier to focus on short-term thinking and safe topics. This often occurs because for some board members, strategy development is not a part of their career or training. And, many times, a nonprofit strategic planning exercise is the first time many individuals have been engaged in a formal process of strategic exploration and planning.

There are also preconceived expectations that some board members may bring to a strategic planning process that influence how they initially think and interact throughout the process. Some may consider planning to be an expensive process, not fully recognizing the positive aspects of the investment the organization is making for its future. Others may fear the group hugs and games that characterize some retreats. And others may question the timing of the strategic planning; this is often evident in organizations where planning has been budgeted and then subsequently delayed for a year or more.

Since so many strategic plans fail, it is important to keep in mind the 13—unlucky—and common mistakes found in the formal strategic planning process. Avoiding theses mistakes will help ensure a strategic plan is well crafted and is well positioned for implementation.

1. Annual Planning
A strategic plan should span multiple years. With the increased speed of technological, environmental, and societal change, many organizations are shifting from decade-long plans to shorter, more nimble 3- to 5-year plans. Also, creating a multi-year plan rather than a new plan every year reduces the likelihood that it will become

associated with the current chief elected officer. Multi-year plans also inspire board members and staff to think beyond the current year and explore the long-term impacts of their decisions as well as potential future changes to the organization and profession or industry it serves. Finally, once the plan is created, it should be considered rolling for a period of at least three years to guide the board, with the organization selecting a limited number of priorities from the plan each year. Throughout this time, the board should conduct a formal annual review of the plan, along with regular review of progress being made on strategic priorities selected for implementation during the current year. The board and staff should also continually look for unforeseen circumstances that may require changes to the plan or to strategic priorities prior to scheduled reviews of the plan.

2. Too Many Planners
Strategic planning is a primary responsibility of a board of directors, given the board's role in governance of an organization. The appropriate size of a board of directors has sparked much discussion in the nonprofit sector. Generally, the size of a nonprofit board should be the smallest possible that allows for meaningful strategic conversations and diversity of thought. Too few people may limit ideas, while too large of a group may draw out meetings with so many people providing input. The dynamics are far different for a group of 15 people versus 30 or 40. If additional input or perspectives are needed for effective planning, organizational leaders should conduct advance focus groups or surveys. Keep in mind, that for every four additional people at a planning meeting, it is likely to add an hour to the schedule.

3. Poor Meeting Environment
The environment in which we operate affects how we think and engage with others. From temperature to natural light, the room environment is critical. Squeezing too many people into a dimly lit room will have a negative impact on outcomes. Avoid basements and dark or narrow rooms, and be sure the room temperature can be controlled. There should also be adequate space for small group

work as well as full group discussion, and additional room for the group to take breaks.

4. Poor Seating and Table Arrangement

Just as the physical aspects of a room affect people, so does the way in which tables and seats are arranged. It is critically important that tables and chairs in a room used for strategic planning be arranged in a way that allows everyone to easily see and hear everyone. Observing body language is key in strategy development, as people often subconsciously exhibit body language that provides a more full context of what they are verbally communicating. Consideration of the placement of flip charts, projector screens, and other planning aids used by the group is also important to ensure all participants feel equally engaged in the process.

5. Unclear Terminology

Many of the participants may never have been involved in strategic planning, while others may come from an environment that conducts planning, but uses terms unique to their settings. Understanding and agreeing to the words associated with nonprofit planning is critical. Otherwise, participants may provide input but don't know whether they are offering a goal, strategy, or tactic. Keep a terminology card on the table that defines the key words that will be used during the process, and review the terminology at the start of the meeting. A suggested list of key terms and definitions is on page 81.

6. The Wrong Season

An ideal time for planning is prior to budgeting for the next fiscal year and/or toward the end of the term of service for board directors and officers. This ensures that organizational resources—financial as well as volunteer and staff time—can be most easily allocated and aligned in implementing new strategic priorities.

7. The Wrong People

Engaging the wrong people in strategic planning can doom the process. Strategic planning is a responsibility of the board of directors. Ideally, the entire board should be engaged in strategic planning; however, if the board is too large, a subset of the board may be selected to participate in the in-person planning process. If this is necessary, it is important to craft a group that can exhibit diversity of thought, providing a variety of perspectives that will ensure the strategic plan created is reflective of the needs of the diverse constituents the organization represents. Organizational leaders should also be intentional to include all board members, not just those selected for in-person planning, but also those selected for pre-planning surveys and/or focus groups to integrate their perspective into the planning process.

8. Poor Plan Report

The value of the final strategic plan should not be measured by the number of words or pages. Some of the best plans can be summarized on a business card. The quality of ideas included in a strategic plan is of far more value than the number of words used to convey them. The strategic plan should be written within a few days of the retreat and shared with participants so they can quickly see results of their volunteer time. Avoid adding fluff to the report that includes pages of reports, the environmental scan (strengths, weaknesses, opportunities, and threats, or SWOT), agendas or survey results. Many organizations produce a separate report with this information, condensing the actual strategic plan to its essence—how the organization will create its future. Let this plan stand on its own as a report about how the organization will advance its mission and goals. It will also help the board of directors focus more on strategy over time.

9. The Wrong Facilitator

The facilitator is charged with keeping discussions on track and completing the task at hand—development of a multi-year, visionary, compelling strategic plan. It is best that a facilitator from outside of the organization be engaged. When a member volunteer or staff facilitates strategic planning, participants often believe hidden agendas or bias may be present. Additionally, senior staff and board members should collaborate as participants in the planning process, since they have complementary perspectives and skill sets. When a member volunteer or staff serves a as a planning facilitator, it makes this level of collaboration very difficult, if not impossible.

Identifying a facilitator from outside the organization who fits its culture and understands the art of facilitation will best serve an organization.

10. Wrong Level of Discussion

Strategic planning conversations should be focused on the macro rather than the micro level. One might characterize board discussions at the 50,000 foot level—visionary, strategic conversations that reach into the future. That would position committees at about the 25,000 to 35,000 foot level, and staff at about 10,000 foot level, implementing the decisions of the board. At strategic planning, conversations should be at the 50,000 feet level and higher. Engaging in tactical conversations can quickly derail strategic concepts.

11. Too Many Goals

Once a strategic plan is created, it is critical for the board of directors to select a limited number of priorities to implement in the year ahead. When implementing strategic priorities, less is more. Organizations can advance their purpose by adopting and implementing a limited number of strategic priorities each year. This allows the organization to successfully implement new programs and services annually that achieve a consistent level of quality.

12. Lack of a Reality Check

Planning should be based on reality. Leaders need to be aware of the capacity the organization has to implement strategic initiatives as well as if the initiatives align with the competencies of its staff, members, and contractors. While brainstorming, it is important to think without bounds, and then during the process of determining how ideas can be implemented, ideas can be scaled to fit with the limited resources of the organization. Strategic planning can be described as the disciplined allocation of resources. Balancing dreaming big and the reality of organizational resources is all part of the process.

13. Improper Deployment

It is not enough to craft a brilliant strategic plan. The plan must also be implemented. It is the process of implementation that causes many organizations to fail. Strategic plans must be integrated into the fiber of an organization. *Strategic Integration* requires leaders to think beyond the planning process and to focus on how they will successfully implement the strategic priorities they have selected. As has been explored in this book, this includes focusing on the following foundations of *Strategic Integration: Simplicity, Creative Communication, Operational Excellence, Maintaining Focus, Absolute Alignment, Iterative Innovation, Systematic Sunsetting,* and building a *Strategy-Driven Culture.*

Strategic Planning Terminology

Familiarization with the terminology used in strategic planning is essential. And developing a shared understanding of the definitions of terms that are used throughout the planning and implementation processes is critical. This decreases the likelihood of potential conflict and misunderstanding that can arise due to individuals using the same words but implying different meaning.

The terms used, and their definitions, may vary based on an organization or consultant's preferences. Following are sample definitions of common terms used, as well as a graphic representation showing how they are linked. Organizational leaders may adopt this terminology or modify it for their use during strategic planning and implementation to ensure a shared understanding of key terms is achieved.

- **Mission**—The reason an organization exists. It should rarely change over time.

- **Vision**—A vivid description of the future, which is inspirational in nature.

- **Values**—Organizational principles that guide decision making and how individuals interact with each other.

- **Goals**—Desired strategic outcomes for an organization. Goals drive an organization toward achieving its mission and vision.

- **Strategies**—Specific programs, services, or other initiatives that advance an organization toward achieving a goal.

- **Priorities**—A limited number of strategies that an organization will focus on accomplishing during a specific period of time. When selecting priorities for implementation, less is more.

- **Tactics**—Steps required to accomplish a strategy. Often written in SMART (Specific, Measurable, Achievable, Realistic, and Time bound) format. Tactics are most appropriately developed by staff.

After the Strategic Planning Retreat: What's Next?

After a strategic planning retreat or meeting, what's next? It is important to quickly translate the discussion and decisions into a written strategic plan. The following steps will help ensure that the written plan is an accurate and useful tool in moving the organization forward as it implements strategic priorities.

Immediately conduct the following activities:

- Circulate the draft strategic plan to the planning group to ensure that it accurately reflects the discussions and decisions that were made during the planning process.

- Share the plan with staff who did not participate in the in-person planning process in order to enlighten them about discussions.

- Seek a motion to officially approve the strategic plan at the next board meeting. (Note that if it is possible for the plan to be written during the in-person planning process, this step should occur before the group adjourns. This will ensure the group's work is not second guessed at a later date, slowing momentum on the consensus that was reached.)

- If no key performance indicators (KPIs), performance measures, deadlines, or assignments were set at the retreat, add them to ensure accountability and implementation. This generally occurs as staff builds a plan to implement the strategic priorities that were selected by the board of directors.

- Develop a plan to promote key aspects of the strategic plan to stakeholders, leveraging the three aspects of

Creative Communication: Storytelling, Mantras, and Visual Communications. This will increase stakeholder awareness and buy-in.

• If the organization has components or chapters, explore with them how it will affect them and how it can be integrated into their program of work.

• Ensure adequate financial resources are allocated and examine any impact to the organization's budget.

• Delegate implementation of selected priorities to the chief staff officer, and empower member work groups and staff to execute next steps.

• Ensure that the board of directors regularly reviews progress on selected priorities.

Within three months, conduct the following activities:

• Ensure all committees and other member work groups are aware of the strategic priorities and direction of the organization.

• The chief staff officer operationalizes the plan,[1] further empowering other staff to take ownership of goals within their areas of responsibility.

• Staff has completed development of a plan for implementation of selected strategic priorities and is monitoring progress of implementation.

• Board of directors continues to monitor progress being made, on a macro level, on selected strategic priorities at each meeting.

At 12 months, conduct the following activities:

• Review the strategic plan, making any needed adjustments to account for unforeseen changes or circumstances.

---

[1] This includes developing a plan to guide implementation of priorities. The plan includes key performance measures, timelines, budget, accountability measures, and assignments.

- Select new strategic priorities from the plan to be implemented during the coming year, and repeat the steps outlined previously.

At 3 to 5 years, conduct the following activities:

- Internal and external environments have likely changed substantially since the plan was developed. The organization should consider developing a new strategic plan.

Engaging Committees

Committees can be considered as business development units of an association. They carry out the vision of the board of directors by working with staff to implement certain strategic priorities, as well as conduct ongoing work of the organization.

If a committee asks, "What should we do this year?" it is a signal that they don't understand their relation to the organization's strategic plan or its ongoing operations. As was explored in Chapter 6, all committees, as well as other member work groups, should have written charges that indicate their role and responsibilities for their term of work. Ideally, these written charges should also include a list of the roles and responsibilities of staff and other stakeholder groups who interface with the committee. Additional information on developing these types of charges is discussed later in this section.

It may also be helpful for committee leaders and members to think visually about the various roles individuals play within the organization. The following graphic may aid in developing a proper understanding of the roles of staff, committees, and the board of directors.

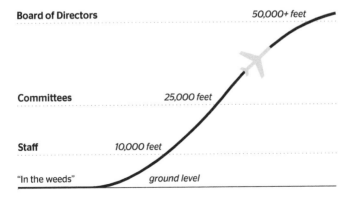

Using the following exercises during the first committee meeting of each work year can help all member volunteers better understand the roles they play and those played by others who are serving the organization.

Committee Charges

Every committee should have a written charge that frames the work it will be doing. As has been previously indicated, committee members should also be aware of the roles staff and other stakeholder groups will be playing related to the work of the committee. Ask committee members to review the written committee charges as well as staff and stakeholder responsibilities and then discuss any questions.

Ground Rules

Committee meetings should have ground rules. For example, "meetings start and end on time; an agenda is distributed one week in advance; the committee works to advance the organization's mission; new ideas and people are respected." Ask the committee members to develop five to seven guidelines that will make meetings more effective.

Strategic Plan

It is critically important for members and volunteers to understand the strategic direction of the organization they serve. Review key elements of the current strategic plan as well as the priorities that were selected for implementation during the current year. Then, engage the committee in a discussion about the importance of the strategies and who in the organization is working to carry them out, as well as any potential impacts to the committee's work in the year ahead.

Sample Committee Chair Orientation

Committee Chair Orientation

This sample committee chair orientation may be adapted for use in a variety of nonprofit organizations. It is a tool that organizational leaders can modify to create a customized program for their organization.

The Big Picture

Serving as a committee chair is a tremendous opportunity to help advance the organization and to advance the industry (or profession) we serve. Throughout your term of leadership, you will also grow personally and professionally. Thank you for your time and your willingness to serve in this role.

Key Policies

Review and discuss the Conflict of Interest and Antitrust policies, as well as other key policies.

Communication

The association has spent a considerable amount of resources developing a brand identity for the organization. This brand extends beyond the association's logo and includes its key message development and modes of communication. In an effort to provide a consistent brand identity, please use staff as a resource when communicating in your role as committee chair to the committee or any other group. Staff should be consulted before sending emails or letters to the committee, the general membership, or others. On the same hand, staff will generally consult you before sending communications if they pertain to your committee. This collaborative effort will result in consistent message delivery and branding for the association.

There may be times when you are contacted by the news media. This doesn't happen often, but when it does, it presents a great branding opportunity for the association. If you are contacted by the news media, first thank them for their interest in the association. Then, refer them to _____ [staff name] at _____ [phone number]. After you have referred the reporter to _____ [staff name], contact _____ [staff name] immediately to let them know about the news media opportunity. The association has a comprehensive communications plan, and referring news media to staff will ensure that the publicity is consistent with the association's communications objectives.

Recruiting Committee Members

Committee membership is open to all members, and all members are encouraged to participate in committees. Committee sign-up information has been sent to all members; however, encouraging new members to join and actively participate on committees often takes more than a letter or email from the association's office. Therefore, in addition to the active members of last year's committee who may serve again this year, *please recruit 5 new members to serve on the committee.* Extend them a personal invitation to join and actively participate in the committee.

The Association's Strategic Plan

The association's leadership follows an annual structure that helps free up member and staff capacity to accomplish the goals in its strategic plan or strategic goals. Quickly accomplishing the strategic plan is vital to the long-term success of not only the association but also the profession we serve. For the association, though, meeting the association's strategic goals is vital to remaining relevant in a quickly changing environment.

While the association is working on its strategic plan, it is important to keep in mind that there is still a strong commitment to the operational work that committees do and for the association's existing programs.

It is also critical for you as a committee leader to understand the major strategic initiatives the board approved for this year:

- Strategic goal 1
- Strategic goal 2

Committee Charges

The board of directors has approved the following committee charges for this year. These objectives provide the framework for the committee's tasks throughout the year. Essentially, the board determines what do to, and the committee determines how. While these objectives provide boundaries, the committee is free to decide how to best accomplish the objectives outlined below.

- Committee charge 1
- Committee charge 2
- Committee charge 3

If goals beyond these objectives arise during the year, it may be possible to work on them. *However, the committee would need to first consult their staff liaison before taking action. The staff liaison will consult with the chief staff officer, who will work with the association leadership to determine the action to take.* This is not meant to restrict the committee. Rather, the committee charges will help each committee focus its work and to work collectively, advancing the organization in a particular direction.

To aid in transparency, you should also be aware that staff are responsible for the following tasks that relate to the committee:

- Task 1
- Task 2
- Task 3

Finance

Throughout the year, it may be necessary to purchase supplies or other items to support the committee's work. It is important to remember that staff can be a valuable resource for you in this regard. Always ask staff to make these purchases for the committee. This will ensure that the committee stays within its budget and will save you time and effort. Additionally, if a purchase is made without staff approval, you may be personally responsible for paying the bill.

Resources

Staff can serve as a valuable resource for you throughout the year. Members have important expertise related to their line of work, volunteer activities, and personal interests. Additionally, staff may provide you with expertise related to their line of work. For example, staff members have professional expertise in event planning, budgeting, communications, meeting planning, etc. Staff may also save you time by offering to provide you with a first draft of agendas and meeting minutes and by sending committee reminders. Beyond that, staff may be a valuable resource for sharing ideas. The role of staff is to be a trusted advisor, a conduit of information for your committee, a link between your committee and the association leadership, and to help you solve problems as they arise during the year. In short, staff is willing to assist you in any way that can help you achieve your goals and grow as a leader.

Committee Succession

Your term as a committee leader is for one calendar year. Each year, the association's board of directors chair appoints committee chairs. Next year, it is likely that the committee will have a different chair and vice-chair. Additionally, appointment as a vice-chair does not imply succession to become the committee chair in subsequent years. This enables more individuals to have the opportunity to serve the association in a leadership capacity. Your time and effort as a leader within the association this year is greatly appreciated.

Meetings

It is generally not necessary for committees to meet every month. Meetings should always have a clear purpose and defined outcomes. We will discuss the general need for committee meetings.

Role of the Committee Chair

The role of the committee chair includes the following tasks:

- Encourage active participation from everyone, realizing introverts and extroverts may respond differently to various types of questions and leadership styles;
- Create a culture of teamwork, cooperation, and collaboration;

- Collaborate with staff to ensure the committee has necessary information and perspectives to make informed decisions;
- Encourage the committee to think beyond the first few ideas or suggestions presented when brainstorming or generating options;
- Express appreciation for everyone's ideas and contributions;
- Encourage differences of opinion, while working toward consensus;
- Evaluate, with staff, how to continually improve meetings and committee performance;
- Ensure the committee stays within parameters approved by the board or executive committee; and
- Celebrate the committee's accomplishments and the contributions of its members.

Role of the Committee Vice Chair

The vice chair facilitates meetings in the absence of the chair. The vice chair can serve in many of the same roles as listed above and has a unique opportunity to assist in ensuring all committee members are engaged and feel appreciated for their contributions.

Specific Activities That Will Make You a Better Chair or Vice Chair

Specific activities that will make you a better chair or vice chair include the following:

- Continue learning about the association
- Devote a part of each week to your duties
- Communicate regularly and openly with staff
- Regularly attend committee meetings and other association events
- Know your duties and fulfill them
- Ask questions
- Be courteous to all committee members

Sample Executive Committee Orientation

The purpose of the executive committee orientation is to review the major principles that guide the group's work and decision making, and review the culture and role of the executive committee and the role of the chief staff officer in light of strategic governance. An annual review of these areas will ensure consistency from year to year. It will also help to annually align the expectations of members and staff and ensure there is a shared vision of the future and of what constitutes success for the association.

Role of the Executive Committee

The executive committee is the servant of the board of directors. It is delegated authority by the board, and may make decisions in between board meetings to ensure consistent focus on the association's strategic plan.

Major responsibilities of the executive committee include the following:

- Ensure there is a common knowledge base for board conversations by determining what data and research should be shared with all board members prior to meetings;

- Draft strategic discussion topics for board meetings, and ensure meeting discussions stay strategic, rather than operational; and

- Approve committee and task force charges.

Successful boards and executive committees conduct the following activities:

- Focus on the macro, strategic level while empowering the chief staff officer to manage day-to-day operations;

- Define priorities and delegate to staff and volunteers for implementation;

- Monitor progress toward strategic priorities;

- Focus on outcomes rather than processes used to achieve goals;

- Create awareness of trends and changes affecting the organization and its stakeholders;

- Consider the organization's capacity and competency when selecting strategic priorities;

- Regularly review programs and services to sunset initiatives; and

- Govern, rather than manage, the association.

Role of the chief staff officer includes the following tasks:

- Help volunteer leadership facilitate strategic conversations;

- Ensure the unique skills, knowledge, and relationships that staff and volunteers bring to the organization are leveraged to accomplish strategic priorities;

- Share expertise and knowledge related to the profession of association management;

- Maintain autonomy to hire, manage, and terminate employment of staff within the parameters of the organization's budget;

- Confidentially set staff salaries and benefits within the parameters of the organization's budget;

- Maintain autonomy to establish office policy;

- Sign contracts on behalf of the organization;

• Align the organization's human capital to achieve the strategic plan; and

• Ensure volunteer leadership considers legal and ethical implications, as well as other important considerations, while discussing and making decisions.

Collaboration

Association leaders and staff bring different and equally desirable relationships, skills, and knowledge to the organization. Members bring a deep understanding of their profession (issues, concerns, understanding of needs, emerging environmental shifts, detailed knowledge of the profession, etc.), relationships within the industry, and a strong desire to engage in meaningful organizational work. Staff members bring a set of technical and strategic skills relating to competencies of association management (facilitation, governance, association best practices, event planning, communications, marketing, etc.) and an understanding of how each committee's work and all staff efforts tie into the overall strategic direction of the association.

The most successful organizations flourish in an environment where both members and staff share, respect, and blend their knowledge, skills, and relationships to do the work of the association.

Throughout the year, the chief staff officer also keeps the board chair and vice chair apprised of issues that may emerge, and key decisions that are made. The three also work closely in handling member-related issues. This fosters collaboration between executive staff and leadership, and also enables the executive committee to maintain its focus on strategic initiatives.

What Constitutes Success?

In many organizations, nearly 90 percent of the association's resources (time/money) is annually devoted to ongoing programs/services and operational needs. Another five percent is dedicated to strategic initiatives; and the final five percent is reserved for emerging issues. As a result, each year, the board of directors defines

two strategic goals for the organization. Achievement of these
strategic initiatives is a large measure of the association's success.

Role Clarity Worksheet

Role clarity helps members and staff effectively work together in serving a nonprofit organization. Three areas are evaluated when determining who (members or staff) should be responsible for doing what: knowledge, skills, and relationships.

The grid below can be used to help create role clarity.

1. List the major tasks associated with an association's program or service.

2. Define what knowledge, skills, and relationships are necessary for each task:

   • **Knowledge:** What unique expertise is required?
   • **Skills:** What skill sets will aid in the project?
   • **Relationships:** What professional relationships would be beneficial to the implementation of this initiative?

3. Determine if members or staff have the required knowledge, skills, and relationships required to complete a task.

Task	Knowledge	Skills	Relationships	Who is responsible?

A Procedure to Vet Ideas
That Emerge During the Year

Overview

When considering adding a new program, service, or project, organizational leaders should explore three general areas: vision, resources, and consequences. (In associations, consideration of new programs or services varies as a primary responsibility of staff, board of directors, executive committee, or hybrid member-staff work group).

Leaders consider the creation of potential programs or services by asking and answering a series of questions in each of the three areas: vision, resources, and consequences—beginning with vision. If the answers to the following vision questions are all positive, the leaders should proceed to the second step, the resources questions. If the answers to all of the resources questions are also positive, then the leaders should review the consequences, both positive and negative, of adding the new program, service, or project.

After carefully considering these questions, the group will be in a position to make a fully informed decision. (If the answers to the vision and/or resources and/or consequences questions are negative, the request should generally not be approved. Also, even if all questions are answered in the positive, there may still be a reason discovered through this process as to why a project would not be approved. Staff should also closely examine the potential timeline for development and implementation, if a request is approved, in order to balance creation of the new program with existing priorities. This may mean that the actual timeline is different than originally anticipated.)

Vision

The following questions will determine if the request supports the association's defined vision.

- Does the request fit with our current strategic plan?

- Does the request support/advance one of our current strategic priorities? If so, which one(s) and how?

- Does the request create value for members and/or stakeholders? If so, how?

- Is the request in line with the association's core purpose?

- Is there currently a similar program in the marketplace? If so, what is our competitive advantage, or what will increase the likelihood of success for our program?

Resources

The following questions will determine if the association has the resources necessary to implement the request.

- Do we have adequate financial resources to implement the request?

- Are there adequate resources among members (committees, task force, etc.) to implement the request?

- Are there adequate staff resources to implement the request (to be answered by the chief staff officer)? If so, how would approving the request affect staff resources?

- Is working with a contractor or outsourcing development of the new program a viable option?

- How would approving the request affect the committee's ability to meet its already established charges for the year?

- If the request is approved, when is the best time to begin implementation? Is it now, or later?

- What do we need to give up or stop doing to implement the request?

Consequences

The following questions will determine the consequences of approving and denying the request.

- Are there any liability concerns? If so, what are they, and how can they be addressed?

- What would happen if we denied the request (both positive and negative consequences)?

- What would happen if we approved the request (both positive and negative consequences)?

- Have we tried this idea in the past, and if so, what were the results? What did we learn? And what is different now?

Program Review Worksheet

This worksheet provides a visual tool for organizations to use when evaluating and potentially sunsetting existing programs and services.

List each program on a separate line. Then complete the following steps individually for each program:

1. Evaluate each program's fit with the mission of the organization.

2. Calculate the increase/decrease in participation during the last three years.

3. Calculate average net income during the last three years.

4. Estimate the amount of staff time required to produce the program.

5. Estimate the amount of member time required to produce the program.

6. Evaluate the Return on Experience, which is based on feedback from participant surveys.

In the table on the next page, enter the following symbols to represent the answers to each of the above questions. (See example on page 63.)

Mission

Yes Program is aligned with the organization's mission

No Program is not aligned with the organization's mission

Enrollment

Adjust the following percentages as needed for your organization:

S Steady +/− 10%

G Growing 10-50%

GG Growing 50%+

D Declining 10-50%

DD Declining 50%+

Net Income

$ The number of $$ represents the size of the profit the program produces.

– The number of – – (minus signs) represents the size of the financial loss the program produces.

Time-S
Staff time:
  H High
  M Medium
  L Low

Time-M
Member time:
  H High
  M Medium
  L Low

ROE
Return on Experience (participant surveys):
  H High
  M Medium
  L Low

	Mission	Enroll	Net Inc	Time-S	Time-M	ROE
Program #1						
Program #2						
Program #3						
Program #4						
Program #5						
Program #6						
Program #7						
Program #8						
Program #9						
Program #10						
Program #11						
Program #12						
Program #13						
Program #14						

Creating an Effective Organizational Ecosystem: Assessment

Organizational Assessment—
Creating a Healthy Organizational Ecosystem

This organizational assessment is designed to create a conversation about the essential foundations of a successful organization.

Each section includes five closed-ended questions. Answer each closed-end question and then ask the following questions to see if your initial answer changes.

- If answered yes, ask: how?

- If answered yes or no: ask: how can we be more effective in this area?

Some organizations discover that some questions to which they initially answered yes are changed to no by asking follow-up questions and engaging in a conversation. Other organizations discover that even though they answer yes to many questions, there are some areas in which they can be more effective. Candid, honest conversation is the key to these discoveries.

Once you have determined if the final answer to a question is yes or no, you may score the question. To score, write "1" in the box next to each question you answer yes and "0" for each question you answer no.

Remember, do not enter a score until you've had a full conversation about the question. After all questions have been scored, add the numbers in each section, and then plot the total scores on the circular grid. Then, connect your dots on the grid and shade in the shape that is created. The areas outside of the shading represent potential areas of growth for your organization. An example of a completed assessment is included in this tool kit.

In addition to scoring this diagnostic, you will also want to keep track of ideas that emerge through the conversation. The real value of the diagnostic is not so much the score, but the insight that emerges, the shared understanding that is created, and the changes that are implemented as a result.

Additional information and a deeper analysis of each section in the diagnostic can be found in the book *From Insight to Action: Six New Ways to Think, Lead, and Achieve*, published by Association Management Press.

Eight Essential Foundations

1. **Purpose** is the reason for an organization's existence and, despite changes to the external environment or profession or issue areas in which the organization operates, purpose represents the one thing that members and stakeholders can never envision changing.

2. **Principles** are beliefs and values that guide an organization's behavior, decisions, and actions.

3. **Potential** is a clear articulation of the future the organization wishes to create. Achievement of the organization's full potential is often expressed in its vision, goals, and aspirational statements. As organizations dedicate themselves to reaching their full potential, they can create positive change in the world.

4. **Processes** are repeatable methods of executing work and making decisions. Leaders function best in organizations that have built processes that result in operational efficiencies and quality outcomes.

5. **Priorities** represent a focused set of initiatives chosen in an operational time frame. Successful organizations select these priorities in light of their purpose and principles, while keeping in mind their limited resources of people, time, and money. Priorities are not about rank-ordering a long list; they are about selecting what to do and what not to do.

6. **People** represents that relationships in an organization should be based on mutual respect and trust, a shared understanding of the roles people play in organizational success. In an association, this includes staff, members, volunteers, and stakeholders; in other organizations, it may be employees and customers or clients, as appropriate to the organization's particular business model.

7. **Praise** represents a genuine, expressed appreciation for the people within an organization as well as individuals served by it. Praise is about celebrating success and valuing the role that people play in achieving success.

8. **Planet** is a clear understanding of how fulfilling purpose achieves positive change in the world around the organization. It means different things for different organizations and should not be confused with environmental sustainability. It is a fundamental awareness that what people and organizations do can have a ripple effect on the communities in which they operate and on the world as a whole.

Purpose		Score
1	Does our organization have a concise, written core purpose and/or mission statement?	
2	Do our board, staff and other leaders have a shared understanding of why the organization exists?	
3	Is our core purpose and/or mission statement visible online and on meeting agendas?	
4	Do we embrace our purpose in such a way that others perceive it in our actions?	
5	Is our core purpose and/or mission statement used as a litmus test in selecting priorities?	

Principles		Score
6	Does our organization have a concise, written set of shared values?	
7	Are all our values shared among board members, committee leaders, and staff?	
8	Do we use our shared values in deciding what the organization should do and not do?	
9	Do we embrace our shared values in such a way that others perceive them in our actions?	
10	Are the organization's shared values visible in our meeting agendas and website?	

Potential

		Score
11	Does our organization have a concise, written, vivid description of the future we want to create?	
12	Does our description of the future leverage our Purpose?	
13	Is our description of the future consistent with our Principles?	
14	Does our description of the future drive our organization toward continual improvement?	
15	Have we created buy-in for our vision of the future beyond the board, with members and staff?	

Priorities

		Score
16	Does the board select a limited number of written strategic priorities to focus on each year?	
17	Are all of our strategic priorities consistent with our Purpose?	
18	Do all of our strategic priorities fit with our association's core competencies and limited resources?	
19	Do we regularly sunset programs and/or services, increasing capacity for new priorities?	
20	Are we flexible in adjusting our strategic priorities if circumstances quickly and unexpectedly change?	

People

		Score
21	Do we align organizational work based on the knowledge, skills, and relationships of members/staff?	
22	Does each committee or task force have written charges, clarifying the roles of members and staff?	
23	Do we value diversity: inborn characteristics, personal experiences, organizational dimensions, style and tendencies?	
24	Do we actively seek and create opportunities to increase diversity and inclusion in our organization?	
25	Do our volunteer opportunities provide for both personal and professional development?	

Process

		Score
26	Does our board of directors engage in an annual process of strategic planning or review?	
27	Do board of directors meetings focus mainly on strategy rather than operations?	
28	Do we have a written policy manual, updated annually, that catalogs the board's policy decisions?	
29	Does the board use both written reports and visual tools to maintain big picture oversight?	
30	Does the organization have written plans for operational activities and strategic priority implementation?	

Praise

		Score
31	Do we routinely celebrate success?	
32	Do we routinely recognize members/volunteers for their contributions to the organization?	
33	Do we routinely recognize staff for their contributions to the organization?	
34	Do we use failures as a way to learn and grow, as individuals and as an organization?	
35	Do we seek opportunities for organizational recognition through external sources? (awards, media coverage, etc.)	

Planet

		Score
36	Do we have a shared understanding of how fulfillment of our Purpose positively affects others?	
37	Do we communicate how achieving our strategic priorities creates a positive impact for others?	
38	Do we look for ways to leverage our programs/services to benefit the larger community?	
39	Are we aware of changing dynamics in the world around us that will affect us in the future?	
40	Do we have a shared understanding of how we are building something bigger than ourselves?	

SCORE

Purpose _____

Principles _____

Potential _____

Priorities _____

People _____

Process _____

Praise _____

Planet _____

INSIGHT

In the space below, write the insight that occurred through the conversation about these organizational foundations. What ideas emerged? How can we be more effective? What changes can be implemented? How can we take these ideas from insight to action?

How Well-Rounded Is Your Organization?

Plot the scores from your Organizational Assessment on the circular grid below. Next, draw a shape inside the circle by connecting the scores. Finally, darken the area inside the shape that was drawn. (An example of a completed grid is on the next page.)

The resulting clear areas outside of the shape that was drawn indicate areas of potential improvement in your organization's ecosystem.

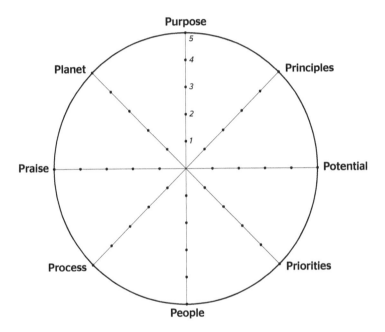

For reference, an example of a completed Organizational Assessment is below, with the areas outside of the shaded shape indicating areas for potential growth and improvement.

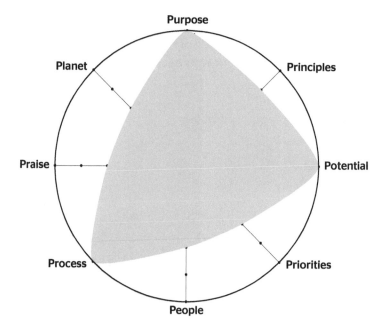

Suggested Reading

Association Operations

- *ASAE Handbook of Professional Practices in Association Management, Third Edition.* John Cox and Susan Radwan. ASAE-Wiley Series, John Wiley & Sons. Hoboken, NJ. 2015.

Governance

- *The Will to Govern Well: Knowledge, Trust, and Nimbleness, Second Edition.* Glenn Tecker, Paul Meyer, Bud Crouch, and Leigh Wintz. ASAE. Washington, DC. 2010.

Leadership and Organizational Structure

- *From Insight to Action: Six New Ways to Think, Lead, and Achieve.* Jean Frankel and Gabriel Eckert. ASAE. Washington, DC. 2012.

Sunsetting Programs

- *Focus on What Matters: A 3-Step Workbook for Sunsetting Association Programs, Products, and Services.* Mariah Burton Nelson. ASAE. Washington, DC. 2015.

Acknowledgments

This book is a collaboration, not just between the authors, but also among many individuals and organizations in the nonprofit sector. The authors first wish to recognize Christopher Oronzi, CPLP, who served as senior editor of this book. His expertise and talent have helped ensure that the publication will make a positive impact on countless organizations and individuals.

The authors also wish to recognize the following individuals and organizations who contributed to the book in a variety of capacities:

Nancy Alexander
Eloiza Altoro-Acevedo, MS, CAE
Lowell Aplebaum, CAE
Holly Bentley, CPLP
Carol Artz-Bucek, CCE, IOM
Susan Avery, CAE
Danielle Duran Baron, CAE
Wendy Parker Barsell
Sarah Berke, CAE
Beth Brooks, CAE
Gregory Brooks
Bill Charney
Edward Cronin, Jr., CAE
Pierre Désy, CAE
Mark Dorsey, FASAE, CAE
Mitchell Dvorak, CAE
Jane Egan
Greg Fine, FASAE, CAE
Jean Frankel
Alison Heron, CAE
Jeff Horn

Wendy Kavanagh, CAE
Vinay Kumar
Elizabeth M. Lucas, CAE
Christine McEntee, MHA, FASAE
Peter McNamara, CAE
Jay McNaught
Greg Melia, CAE
Cynthia Mills, FASAE, CMC, CAE
Jay Millson
Trevor Mitchell, CAE
Jim Moody, CAE
Debra Murphy, CAE
Sarah Murray
Natalie Nardone, CAE
Debra Nolan, IOM, CAE
Anne Ornelas
Christopher Oronzi, CPLP
William Pawlucy, MPA, IOM, CAE
Tim Pyle
Deborah Reeve
Jean Rieden

Brandon Robinson, CAE
Corey Rosenbusch, CAE
Linda Shinn, FASAE, CAE
Scott Steen, FASAE, CAE
Scott Sumner
Sharon Swan, FASAE, CAE
Marty Tomlinson
Celia Trigo Besore, CAE
Lane Velayo, CAE
Dean West, FASAE
Christian Wiggins

AHRA: The Association for Medical
Imaging Management
AMC Source
American Forests
Association Options
BOMI International
Construction Specifications Institute
FarmHouse Fraternity

Florida Academy of Family
Physicians
Florida Swimming Pool Association
Georgia Society of Association
Executives
Green Chamber of the South
Global Cold Chain Alliance
Mind Redesign Consulting
Montana Society of Certified Public
Accountants
Nardone Consulting Group, Inc.
National Art Education Association
New Hampshire Automobile Dealers
Association
Pearland Chamber of Commerce
Set Up Success, Inc.
Synergos AMC
Texas Society of Association
Executives
The Leaders' Haven

The authors also express sincere and deep appreciation to the Building Owners and Managers Association of Georgia. BOMA Georgia has created an organizational culture of collaboration, innovation, and entrepreneurship. And the organization has built a reputation for strategic leadership—and an ability to effectively move beyond strategic planning in successfully implementing ideas and creating value. Furthermore, the entire BOMA International federation has contributed greatly to both authors' understanding and appreciation for the concepts explored in this book.

Finally, the authors thank Baron Williams, CAE; Keith Skillman, CAE; Emily Rabbitt; and the entire ASAE publishing team for their support and guidance throughout this project.

About the Authors

Gabriel Eckert, FASAE, CAE, serves as chief executive officer of the Building Owners and Managers Association of Georgia. He is a Fellow of the American Society of Association Executives (ASAE), a past chair of the Certified Association Executive (CAE) Commission, and a past chair of the Georgia Society of Association Executives Foundation. Mr. Eckert is a nationally recognized speaker, strategic planning facilitator, consultant, and executive coach. Additionally, he is co-author of the best-selling book *From Insight to Action: Six New Ways to Think, Lead, and Achieve,* published by Association Management Press.

Bob Harris, CAE, is an internationally recognized leader in the nonprofit sector, with extensive experience serving associations, chambers, and other nonprofit organizations. He is a widely respected speaker, strategic planning facilitator, nonprofit staff trainer, and board governance consultant. Mr. Harris is a member of the U.S. Chamber of Commerce's Institute of Organizational Management (IOM) faculty, and was named Association Partner of the Year by Association TRENDS. He is author of *Association Management 101 Online©,* creator of the *Association Self-Auditing Process©,* and co-author of *Building an Association Management Company.*